# WRITING HIGH SCHOOL ESSAYS WITH ADVANCED ENGLISH GRAMMAR
## Volume 1

### Quek Boon Chuan

A good expression is usually acceptable:

*"Her eyes were gazing intently because a familiar face had captured her curiosity. She called out to her missing grandfather in a voice that was enthusiastic and earnest."*

A creative expression is really appreciated:

*"Eyes gazing intently, a familiar face having captured her curiosity, she called out to her missing grandfather, a voice enthusiastic and earnest."*

Both expressions are excellent but which is better?

*Determine how you want to express yourself to others so that they can appreciate your written work and give you the merit worthy of your creative expression.*

# Preface

"Students *being saddled* with the task of creating excellent grammatical structures so that marks of distinction can be obtained in the essay writing part of the English Language examination, this ostensibly complex burden is now simplified with an effective, logical and creative approach *intended* to help students gain confidence through a clearer perception of advanced English grammar.

*Being* no less elaborate because of the numerous practices and essential vocabulary lists, this module should enable students to grasp the intricacy of English grammar within a short time, produce advanced grammatical structures proficiently and compose an aesthetic essay, its ultimate aim *to remove* fear and tears from students *struggling* with English composition.

Additionally, teachers and working adults, engaged in extensive teaching or writing respectively, may find this course equally stimulating and refreshing."

Copyright@2005: The author, Quek Boon Chuan, copyrights all materials within the module. Contact: qbchuan@hotmail.com

# WRITING HIGH SCHOOL ESSAYS WITH ADVANCED ENGLISH GRAMMAR
## Volume 1

### Content

| | |
|---|---|
| 1.1 | **LOST IN TIME?** |
| 1.1.1 | Simple and Continuous Tenses |
| 1.1.2 | Simple and Perfect Tenses |
| 1.1.3 | Continuous and Perfect Continuous Tenses |
| | {Self-Practice 1.1 & Assignments 1 & 2} |
| | |
| 1.2 | **PARTICIPLE PHRASES ARE AMAZING SUBSTITUTES FOR CLAUSES** |
| 1.2.1 | Active-Continuous Participle Phrase |
| 1.2.2 | Active-Perfect Participle Phrase |
| | {Self-Practice 1.2 & Assignments 3 & 4} |
| | |
| 1.3 | **WRITING POETIC SENTENCES – MADE EASIER!** |
| 1.3.1 | Nominative Absolute using Active-Continuous Participle Phrase |
| 1.3.2 | Nominative Absolute using Active-Perfect Participle Phrase |
| 1.3.3 | Nominative Absolute using Adjective |
| 1.3.4 | Combination of Nominative Absolutes |
| | {Self-Practice 1.3 & Assignments 5 & 6} |
| | |
| 1.4 | **WRITING STORIES THAT KEEP READERS IN SUSPENSE** |
| 1.4.1 | Suspense & Flashback |
| 1.4.2 | Conversation |
| 1.4.3 | Climax & Conclusion |
| | {Self-Practice 1.4 & Assignments 7 & 8} |
| | |
| | VOCABULARY LISTS |

**Tutorial Assistance:**

This module contains detailed notes and answers with self-practices for students working on their own. However, a teacher's assistance may be required to evaluate the assignments.

# 1.1 LOST IN TIME?

## 1.1.1 Simple and Continuous Tenses

Consider the following correct sentences:

*The florist **carries** bouquets of flowers.*
*The florist **is carrying** bouquets of flowers.*

*The ophthalmologist **examined** the eyes of the patient.*
*The ophthalmologist **was examining** the eyes of the patient.*

*The taxidermist **will stuff** the dead animals to make them lifelike.*
*The taxidermist **will be stuffing** the dead animals to make them lifelike.*

Either the simple or continuous action is appropriate if the context of the event allows it. In this case, always determine the possibility of inserting a continuous action first before choosing a simple action. What is the reason?

*The firemen **scrambled** up the stairs with their heavy equipment. They were soon exhausted on reaching the sixth storey.* (Correct)
*The firemen **were scrambling** up the stairs with their heavy equipment. They were soon exhausted on reaching the sixth storey.* (More Suitable)

Both sentences being correct, the continuous action is more suitable as it pictures the laborious struggle up the stairs, visualizing the action better than a simple action. A simple action reveals the fact that the movement exists, leaving out its continuity that needs not be emphasized. However, there are exceptions.

*Most teenagers **prefer** listening to their peers rather than their parents or teachers.*
*A cyclist **collided** with a pedestrian on the narrow path <u>yesterday</u>.*
*Children **will grow** up and **lose** their innocence.*

A simple action makes each sentence appear distinctly as a statement of fact, habitual fact or universal principle being more relevant than its continuity. It may refer to a single instance or a frequent event happening many times or all the time. Therefore, a simple action is more appropriate, its continuity being not an issue. A continuous action can be described as one comprehensive act too.

*Rioters **burnt** cars in the streets last week. The damages were costly.* [The verb emphasizes the fact of the action.]
*Rioters **were burning** cars in the streets last week. The police could not stop them.* [The verb emphasizes the continuous action.]

Both are correct, depending on whether you want to emphasize the fact or the continuity of the act. Sometimes we just want to state the fact without making the event appear worse than it already is, the simple action having summed up the continuous action comprehensively as a whole single act. Sometimes we want attention to its blatant continuity or aggravating situation, the continuous action having that effect.

**Note: Always choose a continuous action first before deciding whether a simple action is preferable for a mere statement of fact or a habitual action. The continuous action emphasizes movement that is easily visualized.**

Now we turn to situations where the action has to be singular and not continuous:

*The suspect **steps** into a black car and the vehicle **vanishes** into a dark alley.* (Correct)

*The suspect **is stepping** into a black car and the vehicle **is vanishing** into a dark alley.* (Wrong)
[A step is usually a single motion unless it is a slow continuous motion. A slow act cannot be envisaged at that instant. A vehicle cannot vanish slowly as it is either still in sight while fading away or it disappears completely.]

*The plump employer **slapped** the maid once and a struggle **ensued**.* (Correct)

*The plump employer **was slapping** the maid once and a struggle **was ensuing**.* (Wrong)
[The Adverb "once" indicates a single slap. In that context, the struggle follows the slap probably at once or almost immediately and it cannot gradually arise.]

*A bomb **will explode** and **blast** all the glass panes in the hotel lobby to pieces.* (Correct)
*A bomb **will be exploding** and **blasting** all the glass panes in the hotel lobby to pieces.*
(Wrong)
[A bomb explosion is a fast single act and delivers a quick single blow.]

So besides assertions of fact that often require a simple action, there are certain actions that practically must be singular or applied in a single act in most situations.

## Note: Beware of actions that can only be singular in most instances and not continuous.

Having dealt with the Simple and Continuous Tenses in the main clauses, we need to examine how subordinate and main clauses are linked together using simple and continuous actions:

*While the jockey **was racing** the horse to the finishing line, he unexpectedly **fell** to the ground.*
*As newsagents **are selling** the morning newspapers to their customers, they usually **notice** the headline on the front page.*

In the above examples, while the continuous action is happening, the simple action happens **within** the continuous period of time. Notice that the subordinate clause is an Adverb Clause of Time.

*Since the paediatrician **is** only **treating** children, she **will not attend** the seminar on geriatrics tomorrow.*
*As the researcher **was uncovering** a cure for the fatal virus, he immediately **reported** his findings to the authorities the next day.*

In the above exceptions, the simple action happens **after** the continuous action. Notice that the subordinate clause is an Adverb Clause of Reason that includes a continuous action.

Remember that the main clause can also have a continuous action instead of a simple action.

*While the drunken diplomat **was driving** his car recklessly, he **was chatting** with his wife on a mobile phone.*

Consider carefully why each sentence is correct or wrong:

*While the jeweller **was displaying** the diamond rings in a tray, he **spotted** a ring missing.* (Correct)
*While the jeweller **was displaying** the diamond rings in a tray, he **questioned** the customer about the missing ring.* (Wrong)
[The jeweller most probably questioned the customer after he had found a ring missing and not while he was displaying the diamond rings for the customer to view.]

*While the radiographer **is taking** an X-ray of the patient, he **shields** himself behind a protective screen.* (Correct)
*While the radiographer **is strolling** to the X-ray room, he **scurries** towards a patient waiting outside the room.* (Wrong)
[The radiographer cannot stroll and scurry at the same time.]

*While the farmers **will be culling** their chickens on the island, they **will expect** compensation from the government.* (Correct)
*While the farmers **will be culling** their chickens on the island, they **will rear** new chicken.* (Wrong)
[The farmers will not rear new chicken during the culling but most probably after the culling when the threat will be gone.]

**Note: If the Adverb Clause of Time has a continuous action, the simple or continuous action in the main clause must happen within the existing period of the subordinate clause. This may not be necessary if other types of Adverb Clauses are used.**

Having used the same subject in the subordinate and main clauses for the examples given so far, we shall consider a few examples where different subjects exist for the two clauses:

*As patients **are consuming** painkillers to relieve their joint pains, surgery by an orthopaedist **is viewed** as a last resort for severe cases.*
*Since the poachers **were hunting** animals illegally for lucrative profits, heavy fines and even jail terms **did not deter** them.*
*While the auditing staff **will be examining** the accounts, embezzlers **will** still **exist**.*

Observe the two sentences:

*While the toxicologist **was searching** for an antidote, the patient was lying on the hospital bed in a coma.*   (Correct)

*While the toxicologist **was searching** for an antidote, <u>the antidote found by the toxicologist saved the patient's life</u>.*   (Wrong)
[Obviously, the antidote could not be found if the toxicologist was still looking for it.]

The subjects being different for the subordinate and main clauses, the rule as to how the simple and continuous tenses relate to each other is still the same. In fact, it is easier to write correctly with each subject doing only one action than one subject doing two actions at the same time.

## 1.1.2   Simple and Perfect Tenses

Consider the following correct sentences

*Archaeologists **discover** history by digging into the ground.*
*Archaeologists **have discovered** history by digging into the ground.*
[The simple action shows a statement of fact while the perfect action reveals an event that has happened.]

*The croupier **collected** bets and **paid** winners at the gambling table.*
*The croupier **had collected** bets and **(had) paid** winners at the gambling table.*
[The simple action states an event that happened in the past while the perfect action indicates the event had been completed.]

*The furrier **will prepare** the fur for use as clothing.*
*The furrier **will have prepared** the fur for use as clothing.*
[The simple action states an event that will happen in the future while the perfect action asserts that the action will be completed before another possible action will take place.]

No time frame having been given to each sentence such as an Adverb or an Adverb Phrase, either a simple or perfect action is correct and the action itself gives a distinctive meaning to the sentence as already explained.

Now we shall consider each pair of events that have virtually the same meaning:

*The chiropodist **examines** the human foot.  He **prescribes** appropriate footwear.*
*The chiropodist **has examined** the human foot.  He **prescribes** appropriate footwear.*

*The new curator **took** charge of the museum.  Immediately, he **started** an inventory.*
*The new curator **had taken** charge of the museum.  Immediately, he **started** an inventory.*

*Each sergeant **will take** charge of eight soldiers.  He **will guide** them in their training.*

*Each sergeant **will have taken** charge of eight soldiers. He **will guide** them in their training.*

The perfect action appearing redundant in the above sequences, this may explain why students keep using the Simple Tenses without using the Perfect Tenses at all. In practice, writing an essay needs only a few Perfect Tenses especially for Flashback incidents. Similarly, Continuous Tenses are usually used instead of Perfect Continuous Tenses. Therefore, we need to understand the full purpose of the Perfect Tense - a perfect action is a completed action related to another action that happens after it. It being also a past action in relation to a later action, we should call it a completed action rather than a past action to avoid confusing it with a past time frame.

An Adverb Clause attached with each time frame (present, past and future) will clarify the need for calling the perfect action a completed action:

*After the chiropodist **has examined** the human foot, he **prescribes** appropriate footwear.*
[As the completed action happens before a Present Tense or a present time frame, it is called Present Perfect.]

*As the new curator **had taken** charge of the museum, he immediately **started** an inventory.*
[As the completed action happens before a Past Tense or a past time frame, it is called Past Perfect.]

*Since each sergeant **will have taken** charge of eight soldiers, he **will guide** them in their training.*
[As the completed action happens before a Future Tense or a future time frame, it is called Future Perfect.]

The Past Perfect Tense and the Present Perfect Tense can be rewritten as a Simple Past Tense but not the Future Perfect Tense.

*The chiropodist **examined** the human foot a moment ago. He then **prescribes** appropriate footwear.*
*The new curator **took** charge of the museum. Immediately, he **started** an inventory.*
*Each sergeant **will take** charge of eight soldiers. He **will guide** them in their training.*

So calling it a past action can be confusing to a student; it also does injustice to the Perfect Tense that signifies a full completion of the action and not just a past action. The Perfect Tense referring to a completed action like the simple and continuous action and not a particular time frame, we need to add a time frame, thus calling the perfect action a Present, Past or Future Perfect.

**Note: Present, Past and Future Perfect Tenses are all completed actions with each attached to a present, past or future time frame respectively and the perfect action should not be confused as a past action though it may sometimes be rewritten as a Simple Past Tense.**

Confusion with Simple and Perfect Tenses using Adverbs or Adverb Phrases indicating a fixed time are illustrated here:

*The confectioner **brought** the pastries, cakes and other sweet stuffs <u>half an hour ago</u>.*
*The confectioner **had brought** the pastries, cakes and other sweet stuffs <u>half an hour ago</u>.* (Wrong)

*The pregnant spouse **will visit** the gynaecologist <u>in a week's time</u>.*
*The pregnant spouse **will have visited** the gynaecologist <u>in a week's time</u>.* (Wrong)

*The bridegroom **kisses** the bride <u>at this instant</u>.*
*The bridegroom **has kissed** the bride <u>at this instant</u>.* (Wrong)

*<u>Now</u>, the anaesthetist **releases** the sedative gas to put the patient to sleep.*
*<u>Now</u>, the anaesthetist **has released** the sedative gas to put the patient to sleep.* (Wrong)

*The locksmith **promised** to unlock the safe <u>a week before</u>.*
*The locksmith **had promised** to unlock the safe <u>a week before</u>.* (Wrong)

*A public accountant **certified** the final accounts <u>yesterday</u>.*
*A public accountant **had certified** the final accounts <u>yesterday</u>.* (Wrong)

Why should all the perfect actions connected with a fixed time be considered wrong? Besides sounding odd in some sentences, the purpose of a fixed time is to emphasize that the action happens in that time frame. However, the perfect action refers the reader away from that time frame to a completed action done earlier. The perfect action not corresponding with a fixed time in the same sentence, it can be attached to a sentence with a fixed time frame through a subordinate clause.

*The engraver **carved** a name and a design on the metal plate <u>a week before</u>. The plate **was presented** as a gift to the school principal.* (Correct)

*The engraver **had carved** a name and a design on the metal plate <u>a week before</u>. The plate **was presented** as a gift to the school principal.* (Wrong)

*After the engraver **had carved** a name and a design on the metal plate, the plate **was presented** as a gift to the school principal.* (Correct)

An Adverb or an Adverb Phrase indicating a fixed time, e.g. "a week before", "yesterday", "tomorrow" or "last year", accurately fits a Simple Tense rather than a Perfect Tense. Therefore, avoid using a fixed time for a perfect action totally. By now, you should realize that the best place for a perfect action is in the subordinate clause as in the last sentence above, the action in the main clause giving the effect for the cause in the perfect action. Convert it to a Simple Tense if a fixed time is necessary and write it as a simple sentence or a main clause.

*After the courier **has delivered** the parcel, he **returns** with the signed receipt.*
*The courier **delivers** the parcel <u>today</u>. He **returns** with the signed receipt.*
*As the editor **had checked** he manuscript, it **was sent** for publication.*
*The editor **checked** the manuscript <u>a week before</u>. It **was sent** for publication.*

However, leaving out the unessential fixed time and emphasizing the completed action, the Perfect Tense makes a nicer choice.

If an Adverb and Adverb Phrase are not in the sentence to indicate a fixed time, use a Perfect Tense. A period of time fits well with a Perfect Tense.

*The novelist **has written** magazine articles, paperbacks and novels <u>for ten years</u>.*
*The plumber **had repaired** the water pipes <u>for an hour</u>.*
*The brat **will have pondered** <u>for a moment</u> for his misdeed.*
*<u>Since yesterday</u>, the new vegetarian **has not taken** any meat.*

**Note: The Perfect Tense should not take any Adverb or Adverb Phrase indicating a fixed time. The Simple Tense is the exact fit for a fixed time.**

Having dealt with the Simple and Perfect Tenses in the main clauses and also shown some examples of Perfect Tenses in the subordinate clauses, we simply want to focus on the relationship of a completed action in the subordinate clause with the action in the main clause.

Examine the following sentences:

*After the sculptor **has created** a piece of art, he **anticipates** appreciation, not criticism.* (Correct)

*After the sculptor **has created** a piece of art, he **is carving** it for charity.* (Wrong)
[The sculptor is no longer carving the piece of art for charity because he has done it.]

*Since the assassin **had failed** in his attempt to poison the minister, the killer **was silenced** by the mastermind.* (Correct)

*Since the assassin **had failed** in his attempt to poison the minister, he **was told** to do so by a rival minister in the cabinet.* (Wrong)
[The assassin was told to poison the minister before his failed attempt, not after.]

*The survivors of the earthquake **will have received** food and shelter so that they **will not suffer** in winter.* (Correct)

*The survivors of the earthquake **will have received** food and shelter <u>so that they **need** to have them urgently before winter</u>.* (Wrong)
[The survivors will have received food and shelter to survive in winter, which is the intended result, but to have them urgently before winter is simply a reason.]

By viewing the completed action as the cause and the resulting action as the effect, mistakes can be avoided in constructing these sentences. The next examples involve different subjects for the subordinate and main clauses.

*As the usher **had shown** the customers the wrong seats, much confusion **developed** later.*
*Although the psychiatrist **had treated** many mentally unstable patients, madness ironically **overtook** him.*
*Because the stevedores **have loaded** the cargoes into the wrong ships, customers **were** furious with the long delays.*

Have you noticed the cause and effect in the sentences?

*After the chief examiner **had expelled** the candidates from the hall, the students **returned** to the examination hall with their parents.* (Correct)

*After the chief examiner **had expelled** the candidates from the hall, the students **were caught** exchanging written scripts among themselves.* (Wrong)

[The candidates have been expelled after they have been caught cheating, not before they are cheating.]


**Note:  The subordinate clause with the perfect action is the cause for the action in the main clause that is the effect. Therefore, the effect must always come after the cause in time sequence.**

## 1.1.3 Continuous and Perfect Continuous Tenses

The Continuous Tense can also take an Adverb or Adverb Phrase with a fixed time like the Simple Tense but not the Perfect Continuous Tense.

*The teetotaller **was objecting** to the drinking of alcohol in the birthday party <u>last week</u>.* (Correct)
*The teetotaller **had been objecting** to the drinking of alcohol in the birthday party <u>last week</u>.* (Wrong)

The objection to the use of a fixed time with a Perfect Continuous Tense is the same as not using a fixed time with a Perfect Tense. The Perfect Continuous Tense removing the reader from the current time frame and reminding him of the earlier completed action, this completed action is continuous too. So, by definition, the Perfect Continuous Tense is a completed continuous action, being also a cause in the subordinate clause for the effect in the main clause.

*The apprentices **have been crafting** the puppets since young, so they **become** accomplished masters today.*
*The lexicographers **will have been increasing** their vocabularies before they **will** finally **publish** the dictionary.*
*As the explorers **had been combing** the connections in the caves, they **availed** themselves to naturalists and hikers.*

**Note: The Continuous Tense can take an Adverb or Adverb Phrase with a fixed time like the Simple Tense but the Perfect Continuous Tense cannot do so like the Perfect Tense. The Perfect Continuous Tense is best placed in the subordinate clause as the cause for the effect in the main clause like the Perfect Tense.**

In an unusual addition, the Perfect Continuous Tense can imply that the action starts earlier and continues to the current stage of time. The subject may still be doing the action at the instant of the current time frame, being different from the Perfect Tense that is already completed and not continuous. Unfortunately, there is no indication by the formation of the Perfect Continuous Tense itself as to whether it is a completed continuous action or a continuous action that reaches to the current time frame. So it can be ambiguous, leaving the interpretation to the reader, unless an Adverb or Adverb phrase provides the context.

See if you can differentiate them in the following sentences that also involve two different subjects:

*As the journalists **had been asking** too many intimate questions, the popular actor's face **was reddening** with rage.*
[The actor was still fuming so the journalists must still be asking.]

*The somnambulist **has been striding** out of her house and onto the dim road outside, so her parents **are concerned**.*
[The parents are concerned now, so she is still sleepwalking.]

*The composer **has been writing** music for popular singers so that many artistes and fans **do not want** him to retire.*
[The composer may have retired and have stopped writing music or is still writing music and attempting to retire soon.]

Does the fact that the action may still be present in the current time frame affects the inability of the Perfect Continuous Tense to be connected with a fixed time? It does not because the reader is still taken away from the current time frame to look at a continuous action that started earlier or will start earlier.

**Note: The Perfect Continuous Tense is a completed continuous action by definition and yet, in practice, it can also imply an earlier continuous action leading to a current stage of time.**

@@@@@@@@@@@@@@@@@@@@@@@@@@@@@@@

Refer to Self-Practice 1.1 and Assignments 1 & 2 to complete the exercises there before you continue with the notes here.

@@@@@@@@@@@@@@@@@@@@@@@@@@@@@@@

# SELF-PRACTICE 1.1

(These Exercises Should Be Done Before The Assignments. Do Not Submit Them As Answers Are Provided At The End.)

EXERCISE 1: DON'T GET LOST IN TIME! USE TIME INDICATORS SUCH AS ADVERBS AND THE CONTEXTUAL MEANING OF THE SENTENCE TO DETERMINE PRESENT, PAST OR FUTURE TENSE.

**Write one Simple Tense and one Continuous Tense in each sentence.** However, you need to **determine if the formation is Present, Past or Future**. Note that different time frames may mix in the same sentence.
[The *italicized* clues should help! Also, there may be alternative answers.]

Examples:

a.   *While* the elephants **were rampaging** (rampage) into the village, it *was witnessed* that a few wooden houses **collapsed** (collapse).
[Past Tense is indicated by "was witnessed". "While" usually indicates a continuous action. So the next blank should be simple action. It can be determined because the houses could not keep collapsing as observed.]

b.   Paparazzi as overzealous photographers **stalk** (stalk) celebrities to make money. They **are invading** (invade) the privacy of these famous people for the fans' sake too.
[Alternative answers are "are stalking…invade". As the writer, you decide which actions are suitable if there is no Adverb to restrict you. Although there is no italicized clue, the statement is a current habitual fact. So it is Present Tense.]

c.   As the birds **will be migrating** (migrate) because of the *coming winter*, the town folks **will miss** (miss) their sweet songs that they can enjoy today.
[The word "today" is misleading. You should look at "coming winter" to know it is Future Tense. The town folks do not miss the sweet songs today but "will miss" them in future. So "will be migrating" is appropriate. Alternative answers are "will migrate…will be missing".]

WRITE YOUR ANSWERS IN THE BLANKS BELOW:
[Remember to look for the italicized clues.]

1.   *While* the compere _____ (announce) the final winner *that Saturday night*, a participant _____ (*faint*) on stage.

2.   Many local architects _____ (design) such creative buildings that their fame _____ (spread) globally *today*.
3.   During the *last foretelling*, the astrologer _____ (stride) towards his car when pigeon excretion _____ (*hit*) his head.
4.   The author _____ (sign) his autographs at this table *tomorrow*, so the crowd _____ (queue) in the aisle.
5.   A golf ball _____ (*knock*) a caddie off his feet as he _____ (ogle) at a pretty lady golfer in the course *this morning*.
6.   The butler _____ (greet) the guests politely at the door and _____ (usher) them into the main hall when the burglar alarm *sounded*.
7.   The fat connoisseur *did not realize* his wife _____ (be) still in the rest room when he _____ (waddle) towards the exit of the restaurant.
8.   "Her cynical comments _____ (dissuade) the spouse from buying the condominium apartment so you should close the sale fast," _____ (whisper) the manager hurriedly.
9.   Stock prices _____ (move) up and down each day, so anxious shareholders _____ (keep) track of their movements *daily*.
10.  "*Next Sunday*, we _____ (hike) in Bukit Timah Nature Reserve and I'm sure it _____ (be) enjoyable for all of us."
11.  "*A week ago*, bees _____ (swarm) all over the flowers in this garden but *now* we _____ (not see) them anymore."
12.  In the newspapers, controversy _____ (arise) over the death penalty *this time* because a foreign government _____ (attempt) to save the drug courier from hanging.
13.  The mother immediately _____ (*cremate*) the body *three days later* though the youngest son _____ (insist) on a burial for the father but to no avail.
14.  The distinguished lawyer _____ (soliloquize) in his office *when* he _____ (prepare) for a complex case and, therefore, he *does not like* to be disturbed.
15.  *A day before* the accident, a vehicle workshop _____ (repair) the taxi but the taxi driver _____ (take) it back for an urgent use.
16.  An explosion in the chemical factory _____ (pollute) the river but it *is* an accident that _____ (wait) to happen.
17.  "The firemen _____ (extricate) the driver out of the lorry and it _____ (appear) that he is unconscious."

18. "The kidnappers _____ (smuggle) several babies into the country and *sold* them to the adoption agency that _____ (offer) them for adoption to unsuspecting couples *today*."
19. We _____ (receive) high definition television signal transmission *next year* and this news _____ (create) good business for the retailers *instantly*.
20. Several amateurs, who _____ (somersault) to fame *last year*, _____ (perform) again in *this December's competition*.


EXERCISE 2: WHAT CAN YOU DO WHILE YOU ARE MOVING? IMAGINE IF THE SUBJECT CAN DO OR RECEIVE BOTH ACTIONS AT THE SAME TIME.

**Circle the number** on the left if the sentence is **grammatically or factually wrong**. Note that there can be two or more continuous actions in a sentence. Usually there is at least one correct verb but you do not know which one in a single sentence without context. So **underline all the disagreeable actions or indicators** if you can.

1.  While the piglets were scampering away, the hungry foxes ate them.
2.  As examination students are poring over their books, the latest shows in the cinema theatres do not excite them.
3.  Though the Japanese lady was mincing along Orchard Road in her kimono, it does not seem to attract much attention.
4.  The snake was slithering along the drain when it crossed the open grass patch.
5.  The fugitive, whom the undercover narcotics detectives were stalking, slunk into a dark alley.
6.  The little child, who will be inheriting a great fortune soon, is still unaware of his prosperous future.
7.  While the fake officer was prowling in the air base, the base sergeant on duty questioned the man's identity.
8.  Clowns will be prancing into the circus ring as the band was playing a lively tune.
9.  Although the murderer was scurrying towards the exits of the airport, the police arrested him and sentenced him to death.
10. The mysterious lady was leering at a handsome gentleman in the café but he did not reciprocate her gestures.

11. Many public accountants attend the local conference next quarter even though they will be very busy preparing financial statements for companies.
12. While the archaeologists were celebrating their new discovery with the workers, they flew back to Germany to broadcast their findings.
13. The pest control experts are ridding the whole block of apartments of termites, so the residents have to live with the inconveniences.
14. As the geologist was stamping on the ground, he was falling into a deep hole.
15. If the greengrocer is selling rotten vegetables and fruits, he will be out of business soon.
16. Most villagers will be defending themselves against the insurgents as they are living near the border.
17. "The amok was stabbing my colleague once and he bled to death right there."
18. As bargain hunters will be promenading into the exposition hall for the clearance sale this weekend, cash registers ring continuously.
19. Construction labourers are shambling along the streets of Little India and were creating traffic jams.
20. While transvestites are swaggering along the dimly lit streets, undercover detectives are investigating drug activities in the dark corners

EXERCISE 3: YOU HAVE THE POWER TO KEEP THE ACTION MOVING!

**Transform one or both of the sentences into continuous action clause where appropriate** and **combine them as one sentence**. Write both Simple and Continuous actions in the main clause using a slash "/" if both are suitable. Use "while" or any connector to combine them but ensure that the subordinate clause contains a continuous action.

Examples:

1. The old magician shuffles into the hall. He remembers how the audience applauds for him.
*Answer: 1. While the old magician **is shuffling** into the hall, he remembers how the audience **applauds/is applauding** for him.*

2. The wounded hunter hobbled to a hut nearby. He spotted a woodcutter.
*Answer: 2. While the wounded hunter **was hobbling** to a hut nearby, he **spotted** a woodcutter.*
[The verb "was spotting" is not possible.]

WRITE YOUR ANSWERS ON ANY A4 SIZE SINGLE-LINED PAPERS:

1. The engineer operated the new machine. His ears listened for any unwanted sounds.
2. The caretaker checks the floors for any students left in the school. The locked main gate keeps trespassers out.
3. The child will toddle towards its mother. It will look here and there.
4. The drunkard rambles about his miseries. People avoid him.
5. The beggar slouched towards the boy. He glimpsed his son once.
6. The secretary fell when she typed a letter. The back of the chair broke.
7. The culprit paced outside the principal's office. He slipped on the wet floor.
8. The editor bawled out commands. The reporters scooted out of the room for the scoops.
9. Criminologists will study what future prisons should be like. Criminals will still be the same.
10. The firemen are exuberant. They have a week off.
11. The rice farmers protest against the rice import agreement. They suffer from a poor harvest each year.
12. The siren warns people of a coming air raid. It is only a drill.
13. The hurricane may be approaching the islands. We will warn the natives there if it does.
14. The researcher experiments with cloning animals. The scientists enquire about him.
15. Robotics automates the production line. Production workers feel the anxiety.
16. The invigilators eyed the candidates. A few managed to cheat.
17. The property agents scan the newspapers daily because opportunities abound there.
18. The motorcycles often race at night. They anger the residents.
19. The hawkers must sell legally. Otherwise, the environment officers will remove them by force.
20. A driver fumes with rage. He should calm himself down.

@@@@@@@@@@@@@@@@@@@@@@@@@@@@@@

Refer to Assignment 1 and complete the exercises there for submission before you continue with the next exercises here.

@@@@@@@@@@@@@@@@@@@@@@@@@@@@@@

EXERCISE 4: HAVE YOU COMPLETED THE ACTION, HAVE YOU BEEN DOING IT THEN, OR HAVE YOU STILL BEEN DOING IT?

For each paragraph, **write one Simple Tense, one Continuous Tense, one Perfect Tense and one Perfect Continuous Tense**. However, you need to **determine if the formation is Present, Past or Future**. Note that different time frames may mix in the same sentence.
[The `italicized` clues should help! Also, there may be alternative answers.]

Examples:

a. Jacob **prevented** (prevent) a snatch theft `yesterday` while he **was waddling** (waddle) along a quiet street. He **had noticed** (notice) a suspicious character who **had been tailing** (tail) an old lady `for a few minutes`.
[The fixed time "yesterday" indicates a Past Tense and also a Simple or Continuous action. Since "while" takes a Continuous action, the first blank should be Simple. Actions in the next two blanks happened before the first sentence and they should be Perfect action. You can "notice" once but to "tail" someone takes a continuous action.]

b. `Occasional` warehouse sales usually **attract** (attract) bargain hunters who **are seeking** (seek) quality products at lower prices `continually`. These astute shoppers **have been saving** (save) up for the big purchases `for some months` and **have revealed** (reveal) tremendous patience in waiting for the kill.
[Simple action "attract" fits well with "occasional" events rather than "are attracting" which suits continual events. So the next blank takes a continuous action though it can be simple too. Perfect action describes the next sentence because both actions should happen before the first sentence. Perfect action "have revealed" sums up the Perfect Continuous action "have been saving" better instead of vice versa.]

c. `Next month`, survivors of the earthquake **will be trudging** (trudge) back to their damaged towns. It **will be** (be) a logistic nightmare soon. `By then`, he government with international aid **will have provided** (provided) temporary shelters and **will have been rebuilding** (rebuild) homes for them in the ruined areas.
["Next month" indicates a Future Tense. There is no Future Continuous Tense for a being verb that may look like "will be being". So the first blank should be Future Continuous. Temporary shelters should be completed before the rebuilding of homes which is a continual process.]

WRITE YOUR ANSWERS IN THE BLANKS BELOW:

1. *In the previous war, a long column* of soldiers _____ (stagger) *ceaselessly* back from the frontline of which many _____ (be) without limb or sanity. As they _____ (volunteer) as heroes, they _____ (fight) courageously for their country without concern for their body or life.

2. "The firemen _____ (scramble) into the blazing building through the open windows *right now*. I _____ (believe) they _____ (train) for this incredible situation and _____ (prepare) to sacrifice their lives in the hope of saving some victims."

3. "*While* the parents _____ (watch) television in the chalet this weekend, the children _____ (swim) in the pool and *jabber* among themselves. As usual, we, as capable youths, _____ (stock) up supplies for the weekend chalet *till Friday* as we _____ (cook) a big dinner before their arrival."

4. As the eye specialist _____ (peer) into the patient's eyes *for a while*, he _____ (observe) large cataracts in both eyes *and* cautiously *suggested* surgery. *For the past few weeks*, the daughter *had noticed* that her father _____ (squint) because he _____ (be) unable to see further than a metre.

5. *Last Sunday*, the latest office wear displayed in the window _____ (capture) the eyes of a Japanese tourist *while* she _____ (promenade) in the shopping mall. She _____ (hunt) for new clothes to appear trendy and yet professional but _____ (fail) so far.

6. *After* several scientists _____ (initiate) stem cell research, cloning of animals and human limbs _____ (become) popular *today*. Though debates _____ (continue) *for the past few years*, research *still* _____ (carry) on.

7. Athletes _____ (compete) in the *coming* Olympics for goodwill among countries in the hope that there _____ (be) no more wars *in future*. Terrorism and doping _____ (mar) the spirit of the Olympics but countries _____ (strive) *relentlessly* to overcome these blemishes.

8. Computers _____ (dominate) our lives *till today*. We _____ (not know) if we _____ (programme) them actually since they _____ (place) us within their intricate control.

9. Natural disasters _____ (extinguish) many lives within a few minutes or seconds so that life _____ (become) unpredictable these days. Many people _____ (seek) religion for a sense of certainty that _____ (comfort) millions of people for ages.

10. People round the world _____ (protest) against global warming *today*. Governments _____ (appease) them by promoting ozone free products in the community but it _____ (be) inadequate because industries _____ (churn) out harmful gases *since the industrial revolution*.


EXERCISE 5: HAVE THEY COMPLETED THE ACTION CORRECTLY OR HAVE THEY STILL BEEN DOIING IT?

**Circle the number** on the left if the sentence is **grammatically or factually wrong**. Sometimes it can be difficult to determine which words are wrong, so underline all the disagreeable actions or indicators if you can.

1.   After the kitchen hands had washed the utensils yesterday, they wiped them   dry before they put them onto the shelves.
2.   The hotelier has purchased a land site in the prime district as he was building a majestic hotel for tourists with exquisite taste.
3.   The traffic policeman had been scrutinizing the licence plate of a lorry for several minutes as he had suspected that it was a fake.
4.   Visitors were meandering in the night zoo in the dark as the lights had gone   out due to a computer glitch.
5.   The accused had slunk out of the courtroom in the confusion as no one was   watching him.
6.   The auditors were casually ambling towards the building when the bomb had   exploded in the lobby.
7.   After several computer programmers had developed the software perfectly, they had been working hard on it for the past month.
8.   Forest rangers were combing the area for the lost child as they had found him in a cave behind a waterfall.

9. The patient with a backache has visited the physiologist several times though he has been receiving back massages from a Chinese physician.
10. Phlegmatic lawyers will have thought deep into the legal problem before they will come out with a solid solution.
11. Cinema goers will eagerly watch the latest movies so that they will have commented some interesting points about the shows.
12. Companies will have been segmenting the consumer market before they release their new products.
13. Constant hammerings on the upper floor will be disturbing the residents, so contractors will have minimized the noise.
14. Fashion designers have mesmerized their sponsors and potential customers with weird creations that showed creativity more than practicality.
15. Sailors had abandoned their homeland so that they can travel round the world with food and lodging provided.
16. Audiophiles upgrade audio equipments constantly, so dealers have been luring them with the latest inventions to make sounds more realistic.
17. The leopard, which had escaped from the zoo two days before, returned to its cage unexpectedly.
18. The hot air balloon rose high into the sky as the burner has heated the air inside the balloon.
19. Cherry blossoms have been blooming through the season while many tourists would have come into the country to enjoy the beautiful sight.
20. As the wind has been blowing sand into the grasslands, the desert seems to be widening.


EXERCISE 6: IF YOU HAVE CHANGED ONE ACTION, MAKE SURE THE REST ARE CORRECTLY AFFECTED.

**Transform at least one of the sentences into a perfect or perfect continuous action clause where appropriate** and **combine them as one sentence**. Use "after" or any connector to combine them but keep the simple (change to perfect if appropriate) or continuous (change to perfect continuous if appropriate) form as given in the sentence. Leave out unnecessary words or rephrase them to suit the sentence correctly.


Examples:

a.	Guerillas massacred the villagers a week ago.  Bodies are decomposing everywhere.
*Answer: a.  After the guerillas **have massacred** the villagers, bodies are decomposing everywhere a week later.*
[Notice that "have massacred" cannot be in the same sentence as "a week ago", so we move the Adverb Phrase to the Present Continuous Tense "are decomposing" and rephrase it as "a week later".]

b.	Liquefied natural gas is an alternative source of energy.  Huge bunkers on an island are storing the gas.
*Answer: b.   Huge bunkers on an island **have been storing** the liquefied natural gas, which is an alternative source of energy.*

WRITE YOUR ANSWERS ON ANY A4 SIZE SINGLE-LINED PAPERS:

1.	The mountain climber was clutching the rope tightly all the while.  He pulled himself out of the ravine.
2.	The sales representative clinched a lucrative deal from a wealthy industrialist the previous day.  So he celebrated with his colleagues.
3.	The committee was grappling with the problem of the missing fund.  It resolved to suspend the treasurer until the auditor finishes his investigation.
4.	"The crippled dog will limp to its owner.  We shall know the owner then and compensate him for the injury."
5.	A few teenagers hoped to find something valuable.  Therefore, they rambled in the tunnel of the abandoned mine.
6.	Some hungry students were scurrying along the corridor just now.  The discipline master apprehended them.
7.	Several retailers complained to the Member of Parliament a week before.  The upgrading was affecting their business then.
8.	They cruelly buried concubines alive with the dead emperor.  He could have their company in the heavenly kingdom.
9.	The tour agency collected payments for tours.  This is outrageous since it is closing down soon.
10.	The motorist suddenly sped off.  The traffic policeman was ambling towards it at that instant.
11.	The sergeant assembled the recruits before him.  He bellowed at them for trudging back from the cookhouse in a disorderly manner.
12.	The lunchtime crowd of spectators was gaping at the 'spider man'.  He was crawling down the building.
13.	The red rashes infected most of the children in the kindergarten a week before.  It had to close down.

14. The piece of golden wire became an ornament. The craftsman was manipulating it earlier.
15. The dam is providing hydro-electricity to the city. A drought will throw the city into darkness.
16. The debaters were witty and quick to respond to the rivals' arguments. That impresses the judges.
17. A saboteur swiped the guard's head. It knocked him out.
18. Whales are nudging one another to show affection. They are usually in the deep dark waters.
19. The snatch thief wrested a lady's handbag. He scooted into the crowded market.
20. The amok was wielding a chopper. He was chasing the customers out of the restaurant.

@@@@@@@@@@@@@@@@@@@@@@@@@@@@@@

Check the answers at the end. Refer to Assignment 2 and complete the exercises there for submission.

@@@@@@@@@@@@@@@@@@@@@@@@@@@@@@

# Answers for Self-Practice 1.1

## EXERCISE 1

If you get any answers wrong, study the *italicized indicators* or the contextual meaning of the sentence carefully.

1. was announcing…fainted  2. design…is spreading / are designing…spreads  3. was striding…hit  4. will sign…will be queuing / will be signing…will queue  5. knocked…was ogling  6. greeted…was ushering  7. was…was waddling  8. are dissuading…whispered  9. move…are keeping / are moving…keep  10. shall be hiking…will be  11. were swarming…do not see  12. arises…is attempting  13. cremated…was insisting  14. soliloquizes…is preparing / is soliloquizing…prepares  15. was repairing…took  16. will pollute…is waiting  17. is extricating…appears  18. smuggled…is offering  19. shall receive…is creating / shall be receiving…creates  20. somersaulted…are performing


## EXERCISE 2

1. While the piglets were scampering away, the hungry foxes **chased** them.
   [Any correct factual answer is acceptable.]
2. The sentence is correct.
3. Though the Japanese lady was mincing along Orchard Road in her kimono, it **did not seem** to attract much attention.
4. The snake was slithering along the drain when it **spotted a rat**.
   [Any correct factual answer is acceptable.]
5. The sentence is correct.
6. The sentence is correct.
7. The sentence is correct.
8. Clowns will be prancing into the circus ring as the band **is playing** a lively tune.
   [The phrase "**would be prancing**" can replace "**will be prancing**" and "**was playing**" will replace "**is playing**".
9. Although the murderer was scurrying towards the exits of the airport, the police **apprehended** him and **detained him for interrogation**.
   [Any correct factual answer is acceptable.]
10. The sentence is correct.

11. Many public accountants **will attend** the local conference next quarter even though they will be very busy preparing financial statements for companies.
12. While the archaeologists were celebrating their new discovery with the workers, **news media in Germany broadcast their findings**.
    [Any correct factual answer is acceptable.]
13. The sentence is correct.
14. As the geologist was stamping on the ground, he **fell** into a deep hole.
15. The sentence is correct.
16. The sentence is correct.
17. "The amok **stabbed** my colleague once and he bled to death right there."
18. As bargain hunters will be promenading into the exposition hall for the clearance sale this weekend, cash registers **will ring** continuously.
19. Construction labourers are shambling along the streets of Little India and **creating** traffic jams.
20. The sentence is correct.


## EXERCISE 3

Note that there may be alternative answers not listed here where either verb can be used in the subordinate clause. Check with your tutor if you are not certain.

1. While the engineer **was operating** the new machine, his ears **listened/were listening** for any unwanted sounds.
2. As the caretaker **is checking** the floors for any students left in the school, the locked main gate **keeps/is keeping** trespassers out.
3. Though the child **will be toddling** towards its mother, it **will look/will be looking** here and there
4. Since the drunkard **is rambling** about his miseries, people **avoid/are avoiding** him.
5. The beggar, who **was slouching** towards the boy, **glimpsed** his son once.
6. While the secretary **was typing** a letter, she **fell** because the back of the chair **broke**.
7. The culprit, who **was pacing** outside the principal's office, **slipped** on the wet floor.
8. While the editor **was bawling** out commands, the reporters **scooted/ were scooting** out of the room for the scoops.
9. Although criminologists **will be studying** what future prisons should be like, criminals **will** still **be** the same.

10. The firemen **are/are being** exuberant that they **are having** a week off.
11. The rice farmers **protest/are protesting** against the rice import agreement because they **are suffering** from a poor harvest each year.
12. The siren, which **is warning** the people of a coming air raid, **is** only a drill.
13. If the hurricane **is approaching** the islands, we **will warn/will be warning** the natives there. [Note that "will" is used instead of "shall" for a promise.]
14. The researcher, whom the scientists **are enquiring** about, **experiments/is experimenting** with cloning animals.
15. Robotics **automates/is automating** the production line so that production workers are feeling the anxiety.
16. While the invigilators **were eyeing** the candidates, a few **managed** to cheat.
17. The property agents **are scanning** the newspapers daily because opportunities **abound/are abounding** there.
18. The motorcycles, which **are** often **racing** at night, **anger/are angering** the residents.
19. Unless the hawkers **are selling** legally, the environment officers **will remove/will be removing** them by force.
20. If a driver **is fuming** with rage, he **should calm/should be calming** himself down.


## EXERCISE 4

1. was staggering, were, had volunteered, had been fighting  2. are scrambling, believe, have been training, have prepared  3. will be watching, will swim, shall have been stocking, shall have cooked  4. was peering, observed, had been squinting, had been  5. captured, was promenading, had been hunting, had failed  6. have initiated, are becoming, have been continuing, carries  7. are competing / will be competing, will be, have marred, have been striving  8. have been dominating, do not know, are programming, have placed  9. have extinguished, becomes, are seeking, has been comforting  10. are protesting, have appeased, is, have been churning


## EXERCISE 5

1. After the kitchen hands **had washed** the utensils, they wiped them dry before they put them onto the shelves.
2. The hotelier has purchased a land site in the prime district as he **is building** a majestic hotel for tourists with exquisite taste.

[The phrase "**had purchased**" can replace "**has purchased**" and "**was building**" will replace "**is building**".]
3. The sentence is correct.
4. The sentence is correct.
5. The accused **slunk** out of the courtroom in the confusion as no one was watching him.
6. The auditors were casually ambling towards the building when the bomb **exploded** in the lobby.
7. **Several** computer programmers had developed the software perfectly **after** they had been working hard on it for the past month.
8. Forest rangers were combing the area for the lost child **when** they **found** him in a cave behind a waterfall.
9. The sentence is correct.
10. The sentence is correct.
11. Cinema goers will eagerly watch the latest movies so that they **will comment** some interesting points about the shows.
12. Companies will have been segmenting the consumer market before they **will release** their new products.
13. Constant hammerings on the upper floor will be disturbing the residents, so contractors **will minimize** the noise.
14. The sentence is correct.
15. Sailors **have abandoned** their homeland so that they can travel round the world with food and lodging provided.
16. The sentence is correct.
17. The leopard, which **had escaped** from the zoo, returned to its cage unexpectedly.
18. The hot air balloon rose high into the sky as the burner **had heated** the air inside the balloon.
19. Cherry blossoms have been blooming through the season while many tourists **have come** into the country to enjoy the beautiful sight.
20. The sentence is correct.


## EXERCISE 6

1. The mountain climber, who **had been clutching** the rope tightly, **pulled / had pulled** himself out of the ravine.
2. The sales representative celebrated with his colleagues the next day when he **had clinched** a lucrative deal from a wealthy industrialist.

3. The committee **has been grappling** with the problem of the missing fund and **has resolved** to suspend the treasurer until the auditor finishes his investigation.
4. "The crippled dog **will have limped** to its owner, so we shall know the owner then and compensate him for the injury."
5. A few teenagers rambled in the tunnel of the abandoned mine because they **had hoped** to find something valuable.
6. Some hungry students **had been scurrying** along the corridor so that the discipline master apprehended them.
7. Several retailers **had complained** to the Member of Parliament that the upgrading **had been affecting** their business and that was a week before.
8. They **had** cruelly **buried** concubines alive with the dead emperor so that he could have their company in the heavenly kingdom.
9. That the tour agency **has collected** payments for tours is outrageous since it is closing down soon.
10. The traffic policeman **had been ambling** towards the motorist when it **suddenly sped/had suddenly sped** off.
11. After the sergeant **had assembled** the recruits before him, he bellowed at them for trudging back from the cookhouse in a disorderly manner.
12. The lunchtime crowd of spectators **had been gaping** at the 'spider man' who **had been crawling** down the building.
13. The red rashes **had infected** most of the children in the kindergarten so that it had to close down the following week.
14. The craftsman **had been manipulating** the piece of golden wire so that it became an ornament.
15. As the dam **has been providing** hydro-electricity to the city, a drought will throw it into darkness.
16. That the debaters **have been** witty and quick to respond to the rivals' arguments impresses the judges.
17. A saboteur **had swiped** the guard's head that **knocked/had knocked** him out.
18. Whales **have been nudging** one another to show affection as they are usually in the deep dark waters.
19. After the snatch thief **had wrested** a lady's handbag, he scooted into the crowded market.
20. While the amok **had been wielding** a chopper, he **had been chasing** the customers out of the restaurant.

# ASSIGNMENT 1

(Submit these exercises for marking and evaluation. Write all your answers on A4 size single-lined papers.)

## EXERCISE 1: SENTENCE-WRITING

**Write twenty sentences using the continuous action of the "Walk" verbs, which is always active, in any time frame as either subordinate or main clause together with a suitable main clause.** The clause having the "Walk" verb can be an Adverb Clause, an Adjective Clause or a Noun Clause. Refer to the "Walk" Verb List on page 117 of your notes. Abstain from copying any of the sentences from the notes, practices and assignments.

Examples:

a. *While the soldiers **were marching** to the frontline, their families broke into tears.* (Adverb Clause)
b. *The electricians, who **are trudging** into the villa, are carrying rolls of wires to fix up the electrical lines.* (Adjective Clause)
c. *The parents will be glad that their son **will be stepping** into a medical school.* (Noun Clause)

[You may find these exercises too simple. Alternatively, you can attempt the Optional Exercise 1 at the end of this assignment to practise a variety of clauses.]

## EXERCISE 2: PARAGRAPH-WRITING

**Write five paragraphs of short sentences using Simple and Continuous Tenses of any time frame in about thirty words each.** The paragraphs are not related and may be narrative or factual. A good example of the narrative paragraph is the paragraph of short sentences in Suspense (refer to page 38, paragraph 2).

Examples:

a.   The dagger **swung** at his right cheek.  He **swerved**.  He **felt** a scrape and then a burnt sensation.  Red fluid **was oozing** out from the wound.  Infuriated, he **lunged** at the assailant.  Both **fell** into the drain.

b.   The water **is** crystal clear.  Dead silence **fills** the air.  Then the leaves **rustle** and the branches **creak**.  A breeze **is visiting** its domain.  Otherwise, no living creatures **roam** there – except Death!

[In case you are wondering what this is, it is a description of a lake filled with water from the acid rain.]

c.   Refugees **will be returning** home.  Water, food and building materials **will be flowing** in from international aid.  They **will build** houses.  Residents **will work** as usual without fear.  There **will be** peace - one day!

## EXERCISE 3:  ESSAY-WRITING

**Write one narrative essay of 500 words** from the following:

1. A heart of gold.  [It is about a person who has great compassion for others.]
2. Overcoming a small crisis in the family.
3. You were on a journey with someone who suddenly became ill.
4. A fiery fire that turned a coward into a hero.
5. A beautiful journey that I went through.

Alternatively, if you prefer, choose one factual essay below instead:

1. How to deal with terrorism in your country?
2. How do you intend to become a millionaire?
3. Should we have the death penalty?
4. Why is there still war in a civilized world?
5. Is it important that young people should know the history of their country?

Refer to Chapter 1.4, page 83, of your notes on Narrative Essay-Writing (we shall be dealing with Argumentative Essay-Writing in Module 2).  Thus far, you have practised writing a short paragraph of short sentences in Suspense.  That is not enough probably. So try to follow the reduced guideline below as close as you can:


# NARRATIVE ESSAY-WRITING (about 500 words)

PART 1:    **SUSPENSE** (3 paragraphs in about 140 words)
Describe action situations only to create excitement and anticipation as the character or characters suffered a dilemma.
      (a)    Use Simple Past and Past Continuous Tenses.

Paragraph 1: Long sentences can be used to describe actions (about 60 words).
Paragraph 2: Short sentences should be used to describe fast actions (about 30 words).
Paragraph 3: Long sentences can be used to describe actions (about 50 words).

PART 2:    **FLASHBACK** (1 paragraph in about 50 words)
Describe the characters and provide reasons as background information for the suspense.
      (a)    Use Past Perfect and Past Perfect Continuous Tenses.
      (b)    Use Noun, Adverb and Adjective Clauses where possible.

PART 3:    **CONVERSATION** (6 paragraphs in about 150 words)
Describe only significant facts that developed an understanding of the issue as revealed by the characters.
      (a)    Use Inverted Commas.
      (b)    Use any Present and Future Tenses in the speeches.
      (c)    Use Simple Past and Past Continuous Tenses in the narration.

Paragraph 1: Introduce the situation involving characters, location and purpose for this conversation. One or two sentences will suffice with some Clauses.

Paragraph 2: *"Don't disturb me!" bellowed the irritated pupil.*

Paragraph 3: *One culprit retorted, "Here comes your heroine." The three students returned to their seats.*

Paragraph 4: *"If I had not intervened,"* asserted the spectacled girl, *"you would have suffered in their hands again. You must learn to stand up for yourself."*

Paragraph 5: *"Unless you were I,"* responded the timid boy, *"you could not understand."* He had to obey his father not to cause trouble in school as he had been a bully in a previous school.

[For paragraphs 2, 3, 4 and 5, actual examples of how to write a variety of inverted commas are given including relevant narration related to each speech.]

Paragraph 6: Show how characters left the scene to end the conversation.

PART 4: **CLIMAX** (3 paragraphs in about 140 words)
Describe action situations only to create excitement and anticipation as the character or characters resolved the dilemma.
    (a)    Use Simple Past and Past Continuous Tenses

Paragraph 1: Long sentences can be used to describe actions (about 60 words).
Paragraph 2: Short sentences should be used to describe fast actions (about 30 words).
Paragraph 3: Long sentences can be used to describe actions (about 50 words).

PART 5: **CONCLUSION** (1 paragraph about 20 words)
Close the story in any creative way to instill in the reader a lingering thought about the characters.

[Certain vocabulary lists are useful in this outline. The verbs from the "Walk" and "Touch" lists are useful in Suspense and Climax. The verbs from the "Say" list are useful in the Conversation.]

# EXTRA NOTE

NOUN CLAUSES:

**What the coach was proposing** was **that the basketball players have remedial lessons after the tournament.** The idea **that they must expend extra time for them** did not go well with the subject teachers. They believed in **what the boys were doing for the school.** They were certain **that a more amicable solution was coming out of the principal's head**. The principal suggested **that teacher assistants should tutor the boys** instead.

ADJECTIVE CLAUSES:

The matter **that the staff was discussing** concerned Mr Money, **whom the principal kept out of the staff meeting.** The duration **while that was happening** made Mr Money anxious. So he went to the canteen **where some students were chattering.** These students **who admired the teacher for his lively teaching** were eager to know the reason **why the school was not employing him the next year.** Actually, the manner **how he was terminated the week before** was unfair. The complaints **the principal received in the Parents Teachers Association meeting** came from some parents at a time **when their children's examination results frustrated them.** Most parents **whose children did very well** were absent in that meeting.

ADVERB CLAUSES:

**Before the students went out for flag donation**, the teachers assigned them **where they should station themselves.** It was necessary **so that too many students did not congregate in the same area. Although much careful planning was done**, several students still jabber in a group especially at the Mass Rapid Transit train stations. This would not happen **if the teachers were patrolling and checking the locations.** However, the collections were **so successful that everyone was too delighted to bother about a slight hiccup.**

OPTIONAL EXERCISE:

Can you write **a paragraph each** as the above with as many different Noun, Adjective or Adverb Clauses in the same paragraph? Try to retain the Simple and Continuous actions. You can submit them for marking too.

# ASSIGNMENT 2

(Submit these exercises for marking and evaluation. Write all your answers on A4 size single-lined papers.)

## EXERCISE 1: SENTENCE-WRITING

**Write <u>ten</u> sentences using the Perfect Tense and another <u>ten</u> sentences using the Perfect Continuous Tense in active mood of the "Walk" verbs in any time frame as either subordinate or main clause together with a suitable main clause.** The clause having the "Walk" verb can be an Adverb Clause, an Adjective Clause or a Noun Clause. Refer to the "Walk" Verb List on page 117 of your notes. Abstain from copying any of the sentences from the notes, practices and assignments.

Examples:

a.  *After the skeptics **had voiced** out their pessimisms, the believers ignored them.* (Adverb Clause – Perfect Tense)
b.  *The veterans, from whom the novices **have been seeking** advice, have demonstrated their skills willingly.* (Adjective Clause – Perfect Continuous)
c.  *The company is certain that its new rival **will have admitted** defeated in the price war.* (Noun Clause – Perfect Tense)

## EXERCISE 2: PARAGRAPH-WRITING

**Write <u>three</u> paragraphs using only Perfect and Perfect Continuous Tenses in active mood in any time frame of about <u>fifty</u> words each.** Include Adverb, Adjective and Noun Clauses if possible. The following paragraphs are not related and may be narrative or factual.

Examples:

a.  *Some villagers, who **had been sending** supplies, **had warned** the helpless old man about crocodiles. The stubborn farmer **had refused** to leave a tranquil setting near the river although his wife **had been squabbling** with him over the matter. She **had left** in frustration; he **had determined** to stay.*

b.  *A company **has manufactured** electronic firecrackers that **have sounded** like the real stuffs. It **has been serving** new businesses in opening launches; it*

***has not stimulated*** *enough interest among the Chinese families so that they* ***have not used*** *them in the homes for Chinese New Year. However, its sales* ***have grown****.*

c.   *The peasants in the countryside* **will have desired** *more political freedom and* **will have been parading** *in the streets for a less authoritative government in a democracy. The middle-class* **will have** *more participation in the governing process and opposition parties* **will have been campaigning** *for a coming election. All these* **will have resulted** *from the decision of the military junta to return power to the people.*

## EXERCISE 3:  ESSAY-WRITING

**Write one narrative essay of 500 words** from the following:

1. Describe an incident when your injury inconvenienced your friends.
2. Write a realistic story about a small child and her/his imaginary friend.
3. Describe an unusual ride you experienced on the Mass Rapid Transit train.
4. Write a realistic story about a rich person who felt poor.
5. Describe how a maid and her employer got along quite well.

Alternatively, if you prefer, choose one factual essay below instead:

1. Describe a local superstition.
2. Water can be a dangerous enemy.
3. The sounds and sights of my neighbourhood.
4. Which aspects of your education will be most useful in adult life?
5. Animals and birds should never be kept in cages.  Do you agree?

Refer to Assignment 1 for your reduced guideline on writing a narrative essay. Now you are able to write short sentences in Suspense and the Perfect and Perfect Continuous Tenses in Flashback. So keep close to the reduced guideline as you will learn more structures soon to make full use of it.

# 1.2 PARTICIPLE PHRASES ARE AMAZING SUBSTITUTES FOR CLAUSES!

## 1.2.1 Active-Continuous Participle Phrase

### (a) Structure and Function of an Active-Continuous Participle Phrase

Look at some examples of the Active-Continuous Participle Phrase:

<u>**Scurrying** across the basketball court back and forth</u>, the players were warming up for their practices.
The plump seamstress, <u>**waddling** past the confectionery</u>, did not notice the aromatic bread on the shelves.
The cautious waiter balanced the two trays of dishes on his hands, <u>**wending** through the obstacles of chairs, tables and customers</u>.

Don't the sentences look quite stylish compared to using subordinate clauses!

Notice the words "scurrying", "waddling" and "wending" which are called Present Participles. The root words "scurry", "waddle" and "wend" are called Simple Present forms. Present in Present Participle does not mean a Present Tense time frame. It is simply a name for a formation. The Present Participles can be found in Past Continuous, Future Continuous and also in Perfect Continuous Tenses. Confusing isn't it? Just remember that Present Participle is only a name for words with –ing ending and happens to be always continuous in action. (Unfortunately, words with –ing endings may also be Gerunds which are Noun-Verbs. Confusing again? Well, Gerunds are subjects and objects in sentences, so they are easily recognized.)

A Phrase consisting of more than one word does not have a full verb to make it a subordinate or main clause. Adding words to a participle without a full verb makes it a Participle Phrase. Since the Present Participle is continuous in action, we have a Continuous Participle Phrase. The formation of the Present Participle is an active form, meaning that its continuous action comes from the subject in the sentence. Therefore, we now have an Active-Continuous Participle Phrase.

Analyze the following sentences:

*The refugees, **scrambling** for safety in the caves, were avoiding the falling bombs.* (Correct)

*The refugees **scrambling** for safety in the caves, avoiding the falling bombs.* (Wrong)

[There is no full verb in the wrong sentence at all, so it is a fragmented sentence.]

*The refugees **scrambling** for safety in the caves, were avoiding the falling bombs.* (Wrong)

[Like the non-defining Adjective Clause that must be enclosed in commas, there must be an opening comma before the word "scrambling" to enclose the participle phrase.]

The Active-Continuous Participle Phrase describes what the subject, a Noun or Noun Phrase, is doing. Therefore, it is an Adjective Phrase.

This is easily seen when the Active-Continuous Participle Phrase is placed after the subject to show what this subject is doing when it does an action in the main verb:

*The chauffeur, **ambling** towards the hotel entrance, spotted his boss.*
*The bouncer, **pacing** in the discotheque, was watching out for any unruly customer.*
*The patrol car, **meandering** through the dimly lit streets, is ensuring peace and safety in the neighbourhood.*
*The crows, **scavenging** for food in the rubbish dump, are unhygienic creatures.*
*The accused, still **pleading** for his life, will hang in a month's time.*

**Note:** **The Active-Continuous Participle Phrase has an active partial verb or a present participle that shows the subject is producing the action and the action is continuous. However, being a continuous action, it takes the same requirements of the Continuous Tense in the subordinate clause but it is a phrase,**

**not a subordinate or main clause. It is simply an Adjective Phrase.**

## (b) Converting Clauses into Active-Continuous Participle Phrases

Any subordinate or main clause containing a continuous action can be converted into an Active-Continuous Participle Phrase. Even a Simple Tense sentence, having the idea of a continuous action, can be converted too.

Look at Adverb Clauses and the converted Active-Continuous Participle Phrases:

to
<u>While the costumier was dressing up the party-goers</u>, he reminded them return the costumes.
<u>**Dressing** up the party-goers</u>, the costumier reminded them to return the costumes.

<u>As the vandal was damaging the playground</u>, he was arrested by a policeman.
<u>**Damaging** the playground</u>, the vandal was arrested by a policeman.

<u>Although the sentries were guarding the main gate</u>, they did not carry firearms.
<u>**Guarding** the main gate</u>, the sentries did not carry firearms.

<u>Because the pharmacist is dispensing the potent drugs</u>, he ensures the safety of customers.
<u>**Dispensing** the potent drugs</u>, the pharmacist ensures the safety of customers.

Main clauses can also be converted when connected with Adverb Clauses:

<u>The stallholders are slaughtering live chickens at the stall</u> so that they can sell fresh meat.
<u>**Slaughtering** live chickens at the stall</u>, the stallholders can sell fresh meat.

*The bartender was sipping wine out of the bottles so much* that he became intoxicated.
***Sipping** wine out of the bottles too much*, the bartender became intoxicated.

As the maestro is satisfied with his understudy, *the former is grinning widely*.
***Grinning** widely*, the maestro is satisfied with his understudy.

Here are some Noun Clauses converted:

The copywriter was overwhelmed with joy *that he was obtaining the Best Copywriter Award*.
***Obtaining** the Best Copywriter Award*, the copywriter was overwhelmed with joy.

*That the chief administrator will be making her rounds soon* keeps the department heads alert in their tasks.
***Making** her rounds soon*, the chief administrator keeps the department heads alert in their tasks.

The complainant was apprehensive in *what he was reporting about the burglary*.
***Reporting** about the burglary*, the complainant was apprehensive.

Now look at Adjective Clauses and their conversions:

The entrepreneur, *who was generating huge profits in his new venture*, made headline news.
***Generating** huge profits in his new venture*, the entrepreneur made headline news.

The hired cruise ship, *which was carrying tourists to the islands*, developed an engine trouble.
***Carrying** tourists to the islands*, the hired cruise ship developed an engine trouble.

The monastery, *which is accepting drug addicts,* draws generous donations from the public.
The monastery, ***accepting** drug addicts*, draws generous donations from the public.

So is the Active-Continuous Participle Phrase an Adverb, Noun or Adjective Phrase? We have determined that it is an Adjective Phrase describing what the subject is doing. Here we can appreciate that the origin of the Active-Continuous Participle Phrase does come from many sources, thus having many opportunities of writing this participle phrase in an essay without writing too many clauses requiring additional irrelevant words.

**Note:** **Convert many clauses to participle phrases but a few clauses are still needed to show a variety of grammar structures**.

## (c)　　Placing Active-Continuous Participle Phrases in Sentences

We shall look at other locations for our Active-Continuous Participle Phrases.

*A draughtsman **sketching** the plan for the shopping mall has reported sick.*
*An arbitrator **settling** the parties' disagreement will give his decision tomorrow.*
*A craftsman **displaying** his violin making skill was attracting passers-by.*

The Active-Continuous Participle Phrases above do not have enclosed commas for they are defining Adjective Phrases, specifying which one of the many people present is described here by attaching a description to the subject for identification.

*The deer are roaming freely in the forest, **living** a carefree life.*
*A wounded bodyguard survived the attack of the bomb blast, **staggering** towards an army vehicle for rescue.*
*The waiter was carrying a tray of dishes on his head, **wending** through the tables and chairs.*

By placing a comma before the participle phrase at the end, the phrase is referring to the subject in the front part of the sentence. Otherwise, the object at the end of the sentence may be doing the action in the participle phrase.

*The speech therapist glared at the abusive taxi-driver not **speaking** a word.* (Wrong)

[Obviously, the speech therapist should be remaining silent as the taxi-driver was scolding her but the missing comma before the participle phrase at the end makes it describe the taxi-driver instead.]

An object can also take an Adjective Phrase to describe what it is doing. In this case, there must not be a comma after the object or before the participle phrase at the end.

> *The subcontractor witnessed his labourers **sneaking** out of the construction site at night.*
> *The restaurateur was pleased to see so many diners **entering** his new restaurant.*
> *The delegates to the international conference will be disturbed to see many beggars **pleading** for money outside the airport.*
>
> *The platoon commander gazed at the soldiers, **slumbering** in the trenches.*   (Wrong)

[The comma before the participle phrase makes the Adjective Phrase describes the platoon commander instead of the soldiers.  He could not be sleeping while gazing at the soldiers.]

**Note:  Defining Adjective Phrases do not need enclosed commas as they identify the subjects.  Also, no comma is required between an object and a participle phrase that is describing the object.  Only place a comma there if the Adjective Phrase is describing the subject instead.**

## 1.2.2   Active-Perfect Participle Phrase

### (a)   Structure and Function of an Active-Perfect Participle Phrase

Look at some examples of the Active-Perfect Participle Phrase:

> ***Having trodden** over the damaged bridge, the engineers concluded that it was unsafe for heavy vehicles to use it.*
> *Wounded soldiers with minor injuries, **having staggered** from the frontline, were sent back after they were hastily bandaged.*

*The union workers at the shipyard protested outside the main gate, **having stalked** away from the negotiation with the management.*

These sentences still look more stylish than using subordinate clauses!

Notice the words "trodden", "staggered" and "stalked" which are called Past Participles. The root words "trod", "staggered" and "stalked" are called Simple Past forms. Many Simple Past forms and Past Participle forms are the same. Past in Past Participle does not mean a Past Tense time frame. It is simply a name for a formation. The Past Participles can be found in all Passive forms of Tenses and also the Perfect Tenses whether Present, Past or Future. Confusing isn't it?

Unfortunately, it is not easy to recognize the formation of a Past Participle like the Present Participle with –ing endings. Most are similar to the Simple Past forms with –ed endings but there are several variations too like "trodden" for the Simple Past form "trod" and "stridden" for "strode". Unlike the Present Participle which happens to imply a continuous action with –ing endings, it is hard to determine anything from the Past Participle form on its own. It joins with other words to imply active or passive action and simple or perfect action. It can even join other words to become continuous. So don't be quick to think that Past Participle implies completed action, especially in a verbal phrase.

Knowing that a Phrase consists of more than one word without a full verb to make it a subordinate or main clause, we add words to a participle without a full verb to make a Participle Phrase. The formation "having + past participle", e.g. "having staggered", can come from anyone of these formations: "has + past participle", "have + past participle", "had + past participle" or "will have + past participle", for examples, "has staggered", "have staggered", "had staggered" or "will have staggered". All these formations are perfect or completed actions. They are also active indicating action has come from the subject in a sentence. Therefore, we now have an Active-Perfect Participle Phrase.

Also, note that a participle phrase does not indicate number, singular or plural, not showing whether it is a present, past or future time frame. The Active-Perfect Participle Phrase is a completed action done by the subject.

Analyse the following sentences:

*The arsonist, **having prowled** into the factory, set fire to the machinery.* (Correct)

*The arsonist **having prowled** into the factory, holding a can of kerosene.* (Wrong)

[There is no full verb in the wrong sentence at all, so it is a fragmented sentence.]

*The arsonist **having prowled** into the factory, was holding a can of kerosene.* (Wrong)

[Like the non-defining Adjective Clause that must be enclosed in commas, there must be an opening comma before the word "having" to enclose the Adjective Phrase.]

The Active-Perfect Participle Phrase is also an Adjective Phrase, describing the Noun or Noun Phrase, and can be observed clearly when placed after the subject.

*A proud prizewinner, **having stridden** up the platform, will smile widely.*
*Many pilots, **having stalked** away from their posts, are protesting against the low wages,*
*The stationer, **having tiptoed** to the back of his shop, spied upon a few young children shoplifting coloured markers.*
*Some passengers, **having slithered** across the wet floor, managed to enter the train.*
*Several marathon runners, **having hobbled** to the finished line, had blistered feet.*

**Note:   The Active-Perfect Participle Phrase has an active partial verb and a perfect action, indicating that the subject has produced the action and the action has been completed. However, being a completed action, it takes the same requirements of the Perfect Tense in the subordinate clause but it is a phrase, not a subordinate or main clause. It is simply an Adjective Phrase.**

## (b) Converting Clauses into Active-Perfect Participle Phrases

Any subordinate or main clause containing a perfect action can be converted into an Active-Perfect Participle Phrase. Even a Simple Tense sentence, having the idea of a perfect action in relation to the next sentence, can be converted too.

Look at Adverb Clauses and the converted Active-Perfect Participle Phrases:

*After the old retiree had shuffled into his apartment, he passed away on the sofa.*
***Having shuffled** into his apartment, the old retiree passed away on the sofa.*

*As the masons have cut the stones, they plod to the building site, pushing loaded barrels.*
***Having cut** the stones, the masons plod to the building site, pushing loaded barrels.*

*Though the umpire will have scampered into the field, he will not start the game so soon.*
***Having scampered** into the field, the umpire will not start the game so soon.*

*If the child has toddled near the burning stove, he will be carried off to safety.*
***Having toddled** near the burning stove, the child will be carried off to safety.*

Main clauses can also be converted when connected with Adverb Clauses:

*The teenagers have slunk out of their house, so they are afraid to be seen.*
***Having slunk** out of their house, the teenagers are afraid to be seen.*

*The geishas will have minced onto the stage so that they will entertain the businessmen.*

***Having minced*** onto the stage, the geishas will entertain the businessmen.
Her mother had struck a lottery since she bought a car yesterday.
***Having struck*** a lottery, her mother bought a car yesterday.

Here are some Noun Clauses converted:

The lady tenant was filled with grief that she had lost her spouse in an accident.
***Having lost*** her spouse in an accident, the lady tenant was filled with grief.
The secretary denied that she had complained about her boss to his superior.
***Having complained*** about her boss to his superior, the secretary denied it.
The stragglers were apologetic in that they had kept the volunteers behind.
***Having kept*** the volunteers behind, the stragglers were apologetic.

Now look at Adjective Clauses and their conversions:

The stewardess who had humiliated an airline passenger was suspended from duty.
***Having humiliated*** an airline passenger, the stewardess was suspended from duty.

The vehicles that have smuggled drugs into the country are confiscated.
***Having smuggled*** drugs into the country, the vehicles are confiscated.

The production operators that will have left the factory after retrenchment may be rehired later.
***Having left*** the factory after retrenchment, the production operators may be rehired later.

So is the Active-Perfect Participle Phrase an Adverb, Noun or Adjective Phrase? We have determined that it is an Adjective Phrase describing what the subject has done. Here we can appreciate that the origin of the Active-Perfect Participle Phrase does come from many sources, thus having many opportunities of writing this participle phrase in an essay without writing too many clauses requiring additional irrelevant words.

**Note:** Convert many clauses to participle phrases but a few clauses are still needed to show a variety of grammar structures.

## (c) Placing Active-Perfect Participle Phrases in Sentences

We shall look at other locations for our Active-Perfect Participle Phrases.

*Competitors **having cheated** in the sports will be disqualified.*
*Student designers **having produced** trendy shoes will have job opportunities.*
*Pessimists **having predicted** negative growth are shunned by optimistic shareholders.*

The Active-Perfect Participle Phrases above do not have enclosed commas for they are defining Adjective Phrases, specifying which ones of the many people present are described here by attaching a description to the subject for identification.

*A large number of pilgrims were endangering themselves, **having crowded** into the square for worship.*
*A few philanthropists have donated generously, **having heard** the plight of siblings.*
*The kleptomaniac will be jailed, **having worn** out the mercy of the court.*

By placing a comma before the participle phrase at the end, the phrase is referring to the subject in the front part of the sentence. Otherwise, the object at the end of the sentence may be doing the action in the participle phrase.

*The arrogant basket players were gloating at their rivals **having won** the trophy.* (Wrong)

[Obviously, the arrogant basketball players should be gloating or staring with malignant satisfaction because they had won the trophy but the missing comma before the participle phrase at the end makes it describe the rivals instead.]

An object can also take an Adjective Phrase to describe what it is doing. In this case, there should not be a comma after the object or before the participle phrase at the end.

*The motorist was honking at the pedestrian **having scooted** across his path.*
*The furious sergeant will be barking at the recruits **having slumbered** during the lecture.*
*The government is dismayed by the news of a martyr **having burnt himself** outside the parliament building.*

*Security forces managed to capture the saboteur, **having planted** an explosive in the missile silo.* (Wrong)

[The comma before the participle phrase makes the Adjective Phrase describes the security forces instead of the saboteur.]

**Note:   Defining Adjective Phrases do not need enclosed commas as they identify the subjects.  Also, no comma is required between an object and a participle phrase that is describing the object.  Only place a comma there if the Adjective Phrase is describing the subject instead.**

**Note:   Is there an Active-Perfect Continuous Participle Phrase? Yes, there is since the Perfect Continuous Tense exists.  However, we shall deal with that in the next module in which passive moods are discussed because we need to explain why a Passive-Perfect Continuous Participle Phrase does not exist.**


@@@@@@@@@@@@@@@@@@@@@@@@@@@@@@@

Refer to Self-Practice 1.2 and Assignments 3 & 4 to complete the exercises there before you continue with the notes here.

@@@@@@@@@@@@@@@@@@@@@@@@@@@@@@@

# SELF-PRACTICE 1.2

(These Exercises Should Be Done Before The Assignments.  Do Not Submit Them As Answers Are Provided At The End.)

EXERCISE 1: AMAZING SUBSTITUTES FOR SIMPLE SENTENCES!

Combine the sentences by replacing the sentence with an underlined verb with an Active-Continuous Participle Phrase without changing the meaning of the sentence.  You must locate the phrase as instructed.  Write the answers on A4 size single-lined papers.

A.    PUT THE ACTIVE-CONTINUOUS PARTICIPLE PHRASE IN THE FRONT PART OF THE SENTENCE.

Example:

a.    The chief examiner <u>accented</u> her displeasure.  She instructed the candidate to cancel the extra answers within a minute.
*Answer: a.* ***Accenting** her displeasure*, *the chief examiner instructed the candidate to cancel the extra answers within a minute.*

1.    The coach <u>admonished</u> the star player for being late.  He told him to join the team practice immediately.
2.    Some witnesses <u>alleged</u> that they saw an abominable snowman.  They gave an almost similar description of the creature.
3.    The opposition does not provide any alternatives to the government policies.  It <u>assails</u> the government in its newsletters.
4.    The shipyard workers refuse to work.  They <u>assert</u> that their wages are not paid on time.
5.    Thousands of villagers are stranded in the remote mountain.  They <u>assuage</u> their hunger by eating animal feed.

B.    PUT THE ACTIVE-CONTINUOUS PARTICIPLE PHRASE AFTER THE MAIN SUBJECT USING ENCLOSED COMMAS.

Example:

b.    The national pole-vaulter demonstrates her agility and grace.  She avows that she is a vegetarian.

*Answer: b. The national pole-vaulter, **avowing** that she is a vegetarian, demonstrates her agility and grace.*

6.   The psychotic killer <u>rambles</u> incoherent statements about the victims. He does not disclose where he kept the bodies.
7.   Envious rival fans tore up the advertisement posters of the new folk singer. They <u>belittled</u> her achievements.
8.   The existentialist philosopher <u>blasphemed</u> against the city's god of wealth. He antagonized the rich merchants.
9.   The detainee <u>blurted</u> out a confession regarding his involvement in the terrorist network. He also betrayed another cell member.
10.  The nurses will draw a fiery response from the matron. They <u>carp</u> about the doctors' arrogance in public.

C.   PUT THE ACTIVE-CONTINUOUS PARTICIPLE PHRASE AS A DEFINING ADJECTIVE PHRASE AFTER THE MAIN SUBJECT.

Example:

c.   "The major <u>bellows</u> at the platoon commanders for their complacency. He happens to be my brother-in-law."
*Answer: c. The major **bellowing** at the platoon commanders for their complacency happens to be my brother-in-law."*
[No enclosed commas exist because the Adjective Phrase identifies the subject.]

11.  A lecturer received a swipe of the janitor's broom. He <u>berated</u> the janitor for his sloppy cleaning.
12.  A mayor <u>censured</u> the welfare centre for not providing meals to the poor. He realized he himself was responsible for the predicament.
13.  Parents <u>condone</u> the mischievous acts of the child. They will lead him to more wrongdoings.
14.  A liberated country wants the dictator back to face the crimes committed in his reign. It <u>contends</u> for his return.
15.  A company spokesman denies that the company is involved in the investigation. He <u>contradicts</u> the statements of the chairman.

D.   PUT THE ACTIVE-CONTINUOUS PARTICIPLE PHRASE AT THE END OF THE SENTENCE TO SHOW WHAT THE SUBJECT IS DOING.

Example:

d.   The military junta <u>decried</u> the award as a gimmick. It considered it as interference in its domestic affairs.
<u>Answer:</u>   *d.   The military junta considered the award as interference in its domestic affairs, **decrying** it as a gimmick.*

16.   The human rights watchdog <u>deplores</u> the wrongful imprisonment of a German tourist. It has initiated a civil suit against the government.
17.   The actress was speaking to reporters at a film awards ceremony. She <u>derided</u> the poor acting in a much publicized film filled with computer graphic animations.
18.   The Indian actor demanded an apology from the media. He <u>disavowed</u> any connection with a criminal syndicate
19.   The government <u>dissuades</u> the press from pursuing the matter of corruption in the police force. It has threatened to sue all parties in the defamation.
20.   Foreign journalists tend to ignore all the facts about the local issue. They <u>distort</u> the truth of the whole event.

E.   PUT THE ACTIVE-CONTINUOUS PARTICIPLE PHRASE AT THE END OF THE SENTENCE TO SHOW WHAT THE OBJECT IS DOING.

Example:

e.   The mother was fuming at the son. He <u>drawled</u> that he was too weak to go for classes that day.
*Answer:   e.   The mother was fuming at the son **drawling** that he was too weak to go for classes that day.*

21.   His insomnia was resolved immediately by the preacher. The latter <u>droned</u> up on the platform about death and sleep.
22.   The High Court judge was listening patiently. The Senior Counsel <u>elucidated</u> the flaws in the complex case against his client.
23.   The report <u>enumerates</u> the benefits of a public relations campaign to improve the company's image. The board of directors has digested it.
24.   The religious organizations <u>will expound</u> the evils that casinos will bring to the families of gambling addicts. They will argue against their establishment.

25. The guests were gradually treading out of the dinner hall. They <u>felicitated</u> the graduates on their successful accomplishments.


EXERCISE 2: ARE THEY DOING IT CORRECTLY?

**Circle the number** on the left if the sentence is **grammatically or factually wrong**. Sometimes it can be difficult to determine which words are wrong, so underline all the disagreeable actions or indicators if you can.

1. The scoutmaster revealed why the campsite was haunted, embellishing the story with invented dialogue and additional details.
2. The mentally abnormal uncle was thundering at the friendly neighbours uttering vituperative remarks.
3. The shepherd explained to the hunters carefully, murmuring about a large wolf stalking his flock.
4. The pianist receives accolades for a fine piano performance, applauding him for the modern renditions of classical music.
5. The customer demanded to see the manager growling at the waitress.
6. "My mother haggling for a ridiculously low price in a wet market was causing me great embarrassment."
7. The Cabinet minister's response, impugning the motive of the union secretary, advised the union members to negotiate wisely instead of fostering adversity against the management.
8. Inciting the teachers to protest against poor educational policies, the popular activist was adamant on holding a street demonstration, imputing blame on the government itself.
9. Lamenting on their falling share price the shareholders were perturbed at the lack of disclosure from the company incurring losses overseas.
10. Hobbling on blistered feet, the explorers finally found an oasis jabbering with joy among themselves.
11. The supposedly injured pedestrian moaning at the roadside, was luring onlookers, pretending to be in great pain.
12. Husbands, mollifying their wives, usually purchasing an expensive gift, expecting them to forgive and forget.
13. My little cousin, mumbling to her mother, desired an ice cream cone having chocolate chips on top.
14. The Prime Minister is glad to have the translator, paraphrasing during his conversation with the foreign leaders.
15. Persisting in his innocence, the suspect did not break down during the interrogation, even enquiring when he could be released.

@@@@@@@@@@@@@@@@@@@@@@@@@@@@@@

Check your answers at the end. Refer to Assignment 3 and complete the exercises there for submission before you continue with the next exercises here.

@@@@@@@@@@@@@@@@@@@@@@@@@@@@@@

EXERCISE 3: MORE AMAZING SUBSTITUTES FOR SIMPLE SENTENCES!

Combine the sentences by replacing the sentence with an underlined verb with an Active-Perfect Participle Phrase without changing the meaning of the sentence. You must locate the phrase as instructed. Write the answers on A4 size single-lined papers.

A.  PUT THE ACTIVE-PERFECT PARTICIPLE PHRASE IN THE FRONT PART OF THE SENTENCE.

Example:

a.  The novice knight wielded a sword for a few months. He was confident in acting the part in the movie.
Answer: a. **Having wielded** a sword for a few months, the novice knight was confident in acting the part in the movie.

1.  The chef wrenched the cap off the bottle of tomato ketchup. He shook it vigorously.
2.  A passer-by tussled with the amok clutching a knife. He suffered some cuts.
3.  The fireman thumped the hysterical executive on the head. He humped the plump body down the stairs.
4.  The insurance agent swished the signed document in front of the clerk. He prated that it was a million dollar premium.
5.  The custom officer rent the bag apart. He discovered drugs within the layers of the cover serving as the cushion.

B.  PUT THE ACTIVE-PERFECT PARTICIPLE PHRASE AFTER THE MAIN SUBJECT USING ENCLOSED COMMAS.

Example:

b.  The sister nuzzled the baby's nose. She chuckled a few gibberish words.
Answer: b. The sister, **having nuzzled** the baby's nose, chuckled a few words.

6.  The old librarian squinted at the undergraduate. She recalled the girl's face.
7.  The marketing expert differentiates target consumers. He develops the packaging to suit each target.

8. The canoeists <u>wend</u> through the huge balloons in the water. They race for the finishing line.
9. The donor countries <u>pledged</u> money for the disaster torn areas last year. They will honour their promise soon.
10. The sports car suddenly <u>swivelled</u>. It was racing against the traffic flow.


C. PUT THE ACTIVE-PERFECT PARTICIPLE PHRASE AS A DEFINING ADJECTIVE PHRASE AFTER THE MAIN SUBJECT.

Example:

c. A professor droned throughout his lecture without visual aids. He will not stimulate his students.
*Answer:* c. *A professor **having droned** throughout his lecture without visual aids will not stimulate his students.*

11. Bird lovers <u>tread</u> across the high bridge. They will return to enjoy a broad view of the treetops.
12. A magistrate <u>issued</u> a caning order for an underage youth last month. He removed the order later.
13. A conman <u>swindled</u> an old lady of a thousand dollars last week. However, he foolishly left his mobile phone number in a wrapping that contained the fake gold.
14. A veterinarian <u>sterilized</u> the stray cats. She returned them to the animal lovers' group.
15. A mechanic <u>smeared</u> the customer's shirt with grease. He purchased a new shirt for him.

D. PUT THE ACTIVE-PERFECT PARTICIPLE PHRASE AT THE END OF THE SENTENCE TO SHOW WHAT THE SUBJECT HAS DONE.

Example:

d. The managing director yielded himself to the commercial crime unit. He defrauded the private company by gambling in the stock market with its cash.
*Answer:* d. *The managing director yielded himself to the commercial crime unit, **having defrauded** the private company by gambling in the stock market with its cash.*

16. In the old western days, the thieves were hanged. They <u>rustled</u> cattle from the rugged cowboys.
17. The sisters managed to rest their aching feet. They <u>chaperoned</u> the kindergarten kids at a fun fair earlier.
18. The father of the victim fled from the town. He <u>aggravated</u> the situation by killing the murderer.
19. The devious student <u>exasperates</u> all the counsellors' effort. He will be sent to the boys' home.
20. The actress <u>endorsed</u> the product in an advertisement. She has to use the liquid soap daily.

E. PUT THE ACTIVE-PERFECT PARTICIPLE PHRASE AT THE END OF THE SENTENCE TO SHOW WHAT THE OBJECT HAS DONE.

Example:

e. The relatives were disappointed with the son. He vexed the parents with his promiscuity.
Answer: e. The relatives were disappointed with the son **having vexed** the parents with his promiscuity.

21. The movie fans were dismayed with the authorities. They <u>censored</u> a fascinating but controversial film.
22. The accident victim's spouse was furious with the magistrate. He <u>acquitted</u> a drunken driver of manslaughter.
23. Several social groups are already treating gamblers. They <u>fell</u> into heavy debts through credit cards or loan sharks.
24. A burglar <u>bungled</u> a robbery attempt by sneaking into an empty house. The police arrested him.
25. The master <u>eluded</u> the interrogators' traps. The disciples were amazed.

EXERCISE 4: HAVE THEY DONE IT CORRECTLY?

**Circle the number** on the left if the sentence is **grammatically or factually wrong**. Sometimes it can be difficult to determine which words are wrong, so underline all the disagreeable actions or indicators if you can.

1. Having coerced the accounts clerks to falsify the invoices the managing director reported a profit instead of a loss that quarter.
2. The foreign diplomats having enjoyed immunity from prosecution, should not gloat over their privilege.

3. Having barricaded themselves in the building, the squatters refused to leave.
4. Having vandalized the vending machine, the mindless thugs broke its glass panel and dented the sides with violent kicks.
5. The priest empathized with the stranger having lost an eye.
6. Having demolished the old hospital, the wreckers checked the surroundings to make sure it was safe before doing so.
7. David Copperfield, a famous magician, having deluded audiences with his illusions receives wide applause worldwide.
8. The retailer, having apprehended a student for shoplifting called her parents.
9. The icebergs, having melted at the poles, increases the sea level.
10. Having erected a monument for the dead heroes, the memories of their sacrifices will not be forgotten.
11. The host was flabbergasted with the delegates, having boycotted the conference.
12. The rising water having flooded the rice fields, is endangering the farmers' livelihood.
13. Having apprehended the culprit, the mischievous student was punished by the principal.
14. Children are delighted with the lanterns having illuminated the garden for them to run around.
15. The kitchen hand racked the shelf violently having spotted a rat at the top.

@@@@@@@@@@@@@@@@@@@@@@@@@@@@@@

Check your answers at the end. Refer to Assignment 4 and complete the exercises there for submission before you continue with the next segment of notes.

@@@@@@@@@@@@@@@@@@@@@@@@@@@@@@

# Answers for Self-Practice 1.2

## EXERCISE 1

1. **Admonishing** the star player for being late, the coach told him to join the team practice immediately.
2. **Alleging** that they saw an abominable snowman, some witnesses gave an almost similar description of the creature.
3. **Assailing** the government in its newsletters, the opposition does not provide any alternatives to the government policies.
4. **Asserting** that their wages are not paid on time, the shipyard workers refuse to work.
5. **Assuaging** their hunger by eating animal feed, thousands of villagers are stranded in the remote mountain.
6. The psychotic killer, **rambling** incoherent statements about the victims, does not disclose where he kept the bodies.
7. Envious rival fans, **belittling** the achievements of the new folk singer, tore up her advertisement posters.
8. The existentialist philosopher, **blaspheming** against the city's god of wealth, antagonized the rich merchants.
9. The detainee, **blurting** out a confession regarding his involvement in the terrorist network, also betrayed another cell member.
10. The nurses, **carping** about the doctors' arrogance in public, will draw a fiery response from the matron.
11. A lecturer **berating** the janitor for his sloppy cleaning received a swipe of his broom.
12. A mayor **censuring** the welfare centre for not providing meals to the poor realized he himself was responsible for the predicament.
13. Parents **condoning** the mischievous acts of the child will lead him to more wrongdoings.
14. A liberated country **contending** for the return of the dictator wants him back to face the crimes committed in his reign.
15. A company spokesman **contradicting** the statements of the chairman denies that the company is involved in the investigation.
16. The human rights watchdog has initiated a civil suit against the government, **deploring** the wrongful imprisonment of a German tourist.
17. The actress was speaking to reporters at a film awards ceremony, **deriding** the poor acting in a much publicized film filled with computer graphic animations.
18. The Indian actor demanded an apology from the media, **disavowing** any connection with a criminal syndicate.

19. The government has threatened to sue all parties in the defamation, **dissuading** the press from pursuing the matter of corruption in the police force.
20. Foreign journalists tend to ignore all the facts about the local issue, **distorting** the truth of the whole event.
21. His insomnia was resolved immediately by the preacher **droning** up on the platform about death and sleep.
22. The High Court judge was patiently listening to the Senior Counsel **elucidating** the flaws in the complex case against his client.
23. The board of directors has digested the report **enumerating** the benefits of a public relations campaign to improve the company's image.
24. The establishment of casinos will be argued against by the religious organizations **expounding** the evils that they will bring to the families of gambling addicts.
25. Gradually treading out of the dinner hall were the guests **felicitating** the graduates on their successful accomplishments.


EXERCISE 2

1. The sentence is correct.
2. The mentally abnormal uncle was thundering at the friendly **neighbours, uttering** vituperative remarks.
3. The sentence is correct.
4. The pianist receives accolades for a fine piano performance, **deserving applause** for the modern renditions of classical music.
5. The customer demanded to see the **manager, growling** at the waitress.
6. "My **mother, haggling** for a ridiculously low price in a wet **market, was** causing me great embarrassment."
7. The sentence is correct.
8. The sentence is correct.
9. Lamenting on their falling share **price, the** shareholders were perturbed at the lack of disclosure from the company incurring losses overseas.
10. Hobbling on blistered feet, the explorers finally found an **oasis, jabbering** with joy among themselves.
11. The supposedly injured **pedestrian, moaning** at the roadside, was luring onlookers, pretending to be in great pain.
12. Husbands, mollifying their wives, usually **purchase** an expensive gift, expecting them to forgive and forget.
13. The sentence is correct.
14. The Prime Minister is glad to have the **translator paraphrasing** during his conversation with the foreign leaders.

15. The sentence is correct.

## EXERCISE 3

1. **Having wrenched** the cap off the bottle of tomato ketchup, the chef shook it vigorously.
2. **Having tussled** with the amok clutching a knife, a passer-by suffered some cuts.
3. **Having thumped** the hysterical executive on the head, the fireman humped the plump body down the stairs.
4. **Having swished** the signed document in front of the clerk, the insurance agent prated that it was a million dollar premium.
5. **Having rent** the bag apart, the custom officer discovered drugs within the layers of the cover serving as the cushion.
6. The old librarian, **having squinted** at the undergraduate, recalled the girl's face.
7. The marketing expert, **having differentiated** target consumers, develops the packaging to suit each target.
8. The canoeists, **having wended** through the huge balloons in the water, race for the finishing line.
9. The donor countries, **having pledged** money for the disaster torn areas, will honour their promise soon.
10. The sports car, **having** suddenly **swivelled**, was racing against the traffic flow.
11. Bird lovers **having trodden** across the high bridge will return to enjoy a broad view of the treetops.
12. A magistrate **having issued** a caning order for an underage youth removed it later.
13. A conman **having swindled** an old lady of a thousand dollars foolishly left his mobile phone number in a wrapping that contained the fake gold.
14. A veterinarian **having sterilized** the stray cats returned them to the animal lovers' group.
15. A mechanic **having smeared** the customer's shirt with grease purchased a new shirt for him.
16. In the old western days, the thieves were hanged, **having rustled** cattle from the rugged cowboys.
17. The sisters managed to rest their aching feet, **having chaperoned** the kindergarten kids at a fun fair.
18. The father of the victim fled from the town, **having aggravated** the situation by killing the murderer.

19. The devious student will be sent to the boys' home, **having exasperated all the counsellors' effort**.
20. The actress has to use the liquid soap daily, **having endorsed the product in an advertisement**.
21. The movie fans were dismayed with the authorities **having censored a fascinating but controversial film**.
22. The accident victim's spouse was furious with the magistrate **having acquitted a drunken driver of manslaughter**.
23. Several social groups are already treating gamblers **having fallen into heavy debts through credit cards or loan sharks**.
24. The police arrested a burglar **having bungled a robbery attempt by sneaking into an empty house**.
25. The disciples were amazed by the master **having eluded the interrogators' traps**.

## EXERCISE 4

1. Having coerced the accounts clerks to falsify the **invoices, the** managing director reported a profit instead of a loss that quarter.
2. The foreign **diplomats, having** enjoyed immunity from prosecution, should not gloat over their privilege.
3. The sentence is correct.
4. Having **intended to vandalize** the vending machine, the mindless thugs broke its glass panel and dented the sides with violent kicks.
5. The sentence is correct.
6. **The wreckers** demolished the old hospital, **having checked** the surroundings to make sure it was safe before doing so.
7. David Copperfield, a famous magician, having deluded audiences with his **illusions, receives** wide applause worldwide.
8. The retailer, having apprehended a student for **shoplifting, called** her parents.
9. The sentence is correct.
10. Having erected a monument for the dead heroes, **the people will not forget their sacrifices.**
11. The host was flabbergasted with the **delegates having** boycotted the conference.
12. The rising **water, having** flooded the rice fields, is endangering the farmers' livelihood.
13. Having apprehended the culprit, **the principal punished the mischievous student.**

14. The sentence is correct.
15. The kitchen hand racked the shelf **violently, having** spotted a rat at the top.

# ASSIGNMENT 3

(Submit these exercises for marking and evaluation. Write all your answers on A4 size single-lined papers.)

EXERCISE 1: PHRASE-WRITING

**Create your own suitable content of the Active-Continuous Participle Phrases of the given words in the locations where these words are placed in the sentences.** Write out the complete sentences on A4 size single-lined papers and underline the Active-Continuous Participle Phrases.

Examples:

a. ***Stagger***, the wounded robber, ***brandish***, warned everyone to stay down.
Answer: a. ***Staggering into the clinic***, the wounded robber, ***brandishing a pistol***, warned everyone to stay down.

b. The refugees **straggle** failed to reach their destination, **raise**.
Answer: b. The refugees ***straggling behind the convoy with military escort*** failed to reach their destination, ***raising fears that they might be harmed***.

[Note that no enclosed commas are required for defining Adjective Phrase.]

c. The staff witnessed the manageress **stalk**.
Answer: c. The staff witnessed the manageress ***stalking angrily out of the office***.

[There must not be any comma after the object if the object is doing the action.]

WRITE OUT THE ACTIVE-CONTINUOUS PARTICIPLE PHRASES AND BE EXTRA CAUTIOUS WITH THE COMMAS.

1. **Glide**, the model presented a beautiful nightgown in pink, **attract**.
2. **Stride**, the tall policeman, **hold**, received a medal for his bravery.
3. The grandfather, **shuffle**, spotted the grandson **play**.
4. Shipyard workers, **shamble**, were inspecting the dishes, **feel**.
5. **Tread**, the mine experts were surveying the ground cautiously, **eye**.
6. The nanny, **caress**, sang a lullaby, **coax**.
7. **Pore**, the candidates are desperate, **compete**.

8. **Discern**, the host invited the stranger into his cottage, **intend**.
9. **Ogle**, the patient infuriated his wife and saw her **stamp**.
10. The aunt, **peek**, was making faces, **amuse**.
11. The hawker **glare** must be angry with him **complain**.
12. **Wend**, the housewives were moving towards the bargain stall, **contemplate**.
13. **Strut**, the champion was elated, **grin**.
14. The overworked surgeon, **slouch**, was chatting with a few nurses, **appear**.
15. **Embrace**, the sisters were in tears, **whisper**.
16. **Slink**, the prodigal son seated himself in the back, **weep**.
17. The disgruntled executive, **babble**, was probably drunk, **cause**.
18. **Foretell**, the fortune-teller noticed the client's face **express**.
19. The supervisor, **intercede**, met the furious manager, **suggest**.
20. A postman **peer** sniffed a terrible scent **come**.


## EXERCISE 2: SENTENCE-WRITING

**Write twenty sentences in which there are two Active-Continuous Participle Phrases each using the "Walk" and "Look" verbs at the end of the manual in any time frame together with a suitable main clause.** You can use the present participle forms of the **"Touch" verbs** instead of the "Look" verbs. The main clauses have to be original and not copied from earlier sentences.

Examples:

a. ***Stumbling** in the dark workshop, the carpenter was looking for the light switch, **peering** here and there.*

b. *The lady on high heels **tripping** into the boutique frequently spends a lot of time in the shop, **eyeing** for the latest branded clothes.*

c. ***Sauntering** into the room, I often see the boys **wrestling** with each other.*

## EXERCISE 3: PARAGRAPH-WRITING

**Write one Suspense of three paragraphs using at least eight Active-Continuous Participle Phrases** (you can lengthen the paragraphs to achieve this) and **one paragraph for Flashback using the Perfect and Perfect Continuous Tenses.** Follow the Narrative Essay-Writing guideline as close as possible.

PART 1:　　**SUSPENSE** (3 paragraphs in about 140 words)
　　Describe action situations only to create excitement and anticipation as the character or characters suffered a dilemma.
　　　　(a)　Use Simple Past and Past Continuous Tenses.
　　　　(b)　Use Active-Continuous Participle Phrases

　　Paragraph 1: Long sentences can be used to describe actions (about 60 words).
　　Paragraph 2: Short sentences should be used to describe fast actions (about 30 words).
　　Paragraph 3: Long sentences can be used to describe actions (about 50 words).

PART 2:　　**FLASHBACK** (1 paragraph in about 50 words)
　　Describe the characters and provide reasons as background information for the suspense.
　　　　(a)　Use Past Perfect and Past Perfect Continuous Tenses.
　　　　(b)　Use Noun, Adverb and Adjective Clauses where possible.

Example:
　　*Firemen, **plodding** up the staircase in the blazing building, were lumbering along with oxygen tanks and tools. Dense smoke and heat **blurring** their vision were hindering their progress. With their oxygen masks on, they were determined to reach the victims on the upper floors. On each floor, one fireman took off his mask, **yelling** out for a response. Then they continued.*

　　*On one floor, a voice blurted out for help. A man, **gasping** for air, was found in the toilet. **Sharing** an oxygen mask with a fireman, he trod down the stairs to safety.*

　　*The rest proceeded to the next floor, **sharpening** their ears for another victim. **Approaching** where it seemed they could go no further, they were* *blocked by ferocious flames **engulfing** the staircase. **Turning** back, they suddenly heard a groan from the upper floor. They paused, **waiting** for a decision.*

*These firemen, whose training **had prepared** them to rescue fire victims without jeopardizing their own lives, **had been pondering** what if they came across a situation where they would have to take a gamble. They **had put** off any decision on this possible scenario. That predicament **had arisen**.*

## EXERCISE 4: ESSAY-WRITING

**Write one narrative essay of 500 words** from the following:

1. A sea rescue.
2. Describe the saddest event of your life.
3. Describe an embarrassing incident.
4. Lost and found.
5. Describe your first experience while riding a bicycle.

Alternatively, if you prefer, choose one factual essay below instead:

1. Should private tuition be necessary for school students?
2. Which identity do you prefer – a national or global citizenship?
3. Describe an unusual custom in your country.
4. Tourism – is it good or bad?
5. All forms of gambling are bad. Do you agree?

You have learnt how to write Active-Continuous Participle Phrases that are useful in your Suspense and Climax. Remember to include what you have practised so far in your essay such as short sentences and flashback. Refer to the same narrative essay guideline if you are writing a narrative composition.

# ASSIGNMENT 4

(Submit these exercises for marking and evaluation. Write all your answers on A4 size single-lined papers.)

## EXERCISE 1: PHRASE-WRITING

**Create your own suitable content of the Active-Perfect (AP) and Active-Continuous (AC) Participle Phrases of the given words in the locations where these words are placed in the sentences.** Write out the complete sentences on A4 size single-lined papers and underline the Active-Perfect Participle Phrases.

Examples:

a. **Slither – AP**, the agile teenager slipped away from the gangsters, **escape – AC**.
*Answer:* a. **Having slithered** under the truck, the agile teenager slipped away from the gangsters, **escaping** their grasp that night.

b. The tycoon, **crumble – AP**, was infuriated with the paparazzi **photograph – AC**.
*Answer:* b. The tycoon, **having crumbled** the tabloid, was infuriated with the paparazzi **photographing** him with his mistress at a resort.

c. **Disregard – AC**, the dictator has strengthened his army and police, **enrich – AP**.
*Answer:* c. **Disregarding** the needs of the poor in the country, the dictator has strengthened his army and police, **having enriched** himself from the diamond mines.

WRITE OUT THE ACTIVE-CONTINUOUS AND ACTIVE-PERFECT PARTICIPLE PHRASES AND BE EXTRA CAUTIOUS WITH THE COMMAS.

1. **Yank – AP**, the technician unscrewed the bolts of the computer casing, **ensure – AC**.
2. The grandaunt, **dandle – AP**, bought her an ice cream, **coax – AC**.
3. **Elbow – AP**, the security guard shoved him to the floor, **caution – AC**.
4. **Extirpate – AP**, the gardener proceeds to add fertilizer, **enrich – AC**.
5. The deceased, **grapple – AC**, was ultimately strangled, **scrape – AP**.

6. The prince, **embrace – AP**, roamed the streets as a monk **collect – AC**.
7. The guests, **reserve – AP**, were eager to watch the famous comedian **jest – AC**.
8. A frightened lad, **stammer – AC**, was suffering from a shock, **peep – AP**.
9. Two chubby boys, **waddle – AC**, out of the barber shop, are twins, **receive – AP**.
10. Several rescuers, **scoot – AP**, were gazing at the distraught miners **stagger – AC**.
11. **Scrutinize – AC**, the interviewers will be probing the job-seekers, **scan – AP**.
12. The lawyer, **reiterate – AC**, was finding flaws with the witness' statements **affect – AP**.
13. **Solicit – AP**, the budding entrepreneur cautiously rents a shop space, **surmise – AC**.
14. **Prod – AP**, the immigration officers continued their search in the dormitory, **anticipate – AC**.
15. **Rive – AP**, the train flew off the track, **plunge – AC**.
16. The native, **wring – AP**, put the body into a bag, **propose – AC**.
17. Some skeptics **scoff – AC** will emerge to see the prototype **fail – AP**.
18. The calm waves **caress – AP** may turn into a monstrous tsunami **drown – AC**.
19. A gossiper **broach – AC** will pay a price for his words **slander – AP**.
20. A dying testator **sputter – AC** cannot change his written will **predetermine – AP**.


## EXERCISE 2: SENTENCE-WRITING

**Write <u>twenty</u> sentences in which there is <u>one</u> Active-Perfect Participle Phrase and <u>one</u> Active-Continuous Participle Phrases in each sentence. Use the Vocabulary Lists** on page 117 as much as you can to know more useful verbs but this is optional. Be original and avoid copying from earlier sentences. However, you can get ideas from them like the examples in Exercise 1.

# EXERCISE 3: PARAGRAPH-WRITING

**Write one Suspense of three paragraphs using at least four Active-Perfect Participle Phrases and four Active-Continuous Participle Phrases** (you can lengthen the paragraphs to achieve this) and **one paragraph for Flashback using the Perfect and Perfect Continuous Tenses**. Follow the Narrative Essay-Writing guideline as close as possible.

PART 1: **SUSPENSE** (3 paragraphs in about 140 words)
Describe action situations only to create excitement and anticipation as the character or characters suffered a dilemma.
    (a)    Use Simple Past and Past Continuous Tenses.
    (b)    Use Active-Continuous and Active-Perfect Participle Phrases.

Paragraph 1: Long sentences can be used to describe actions (about 60 words).
Paragraph 2: Short sentences should be used to describe fast actions (about 30 words).
Paragraph 3: Long sentences can be used to describe actions (about 50 words).

PART 2: **FLASHBACK** (1 paragraph in about 50 words)
Describe the characters and provide reasons as background information for the suspense.
    (a)    Use Past Perfect and Past Perfect Continuous Tenses.
    (b)    Use Noun, Adverb and Adjective Clauses where possible.

Example:

> ***Having discarded*** *the few bottles of alcohol in the chute*, the desperate housewife resolved to keep her once caring husband sober that night, **waiting** *frantically for the outcome upon his return*. However, he might still get drunk at a bar on the way home, ***having celebrated*** *with colleagues* several times after work. He was late, ***indicating*** *he might be drunk again*.
>
> ***Having heard*** *a sudden creak from the front door*, she dropped her cold hands. Her heart was throbbing faster. She must hide from another battering. Her feet would not move. The drunken spouse would find her anyway.

***Emerging*** *from the doorway, a familiar face greeted her. It was the mother-in-law.* ***Trailing*** *behind, the father-in-law sputtered a greeting. Unexpectedly, he was dragging the son back home. The drunkard,* ***having stumbled*** *into the apartment, staggered towards the sofa and reeled onto the floor instead. The parents-in-law simply sat on the sofa,* ***appearing*** *grim.*

*The unassuming daughter-in-law* **had been anticipating** *a stern lecture from the parents because she* **had neglected** *her duty as a wife. His demanding job* **had stressed** *him too much. If she* **had watched** *him closely, he* **would not have become** *an alcoholic. She* **had been willing** *to accept the blame.*

## EXERCISE 4: ESSAY-WRITING

**Write one narrative essay of 500 words** from the following:

1. Write a realistic story about a scary incident in a passenger plane.
2. Describe an occasion when you had to frantically prepare a party.
3. Write a realistic story about how a person fought against corruption.
4. Give two or three examples of unruly behaviour you witnessed.
5. Describe two or three incidents on how some people foolishly lost money.

Alternatively, if you prefer, choose one factual essay below instead:

1. What problems do teenagers in your country face today?
2. Discuss the benefits and problems of retirement?
3. Is e-learning replacing teachers today?
4. Why do people smoke? Do you think it is bad and why?
5. How should a person in huge debt recover from his predicament?

You have learnt how to write Active-Continuous and Active-Perfect Participle Phrases that are useful in your Suspense and Climax. Remember to include what you have practised so far in your narrative essay such as short sentences and flashback. Refer to the same narrative essay-writing guideline if you are writing a narrative composition.

# 1.3 WRITING POETIC SENTENCES - MADE EASIER!

## 1.3.1 Nominative Absolute using Active-Continuous Participle Phrase

### (a) Structure and Function of a Nominative Absolute using Active-Continuous Participle Phrase

Look at some examples of the Nominative Absolute construction using Active-Continuous Participle Phrase:

<u>Their eyes **scanning** the treetops for wild monkeys</u>, the forest rangers had cages ready to catch a few creatures for observation.
<u>The indignant bus driver **bellowing** at a passenger for not paying the full fare</u>, other passengers were annoyed at the delay.
<u>A mother **coaxing** her child to consume the porridge</u>, the twin sisters were amused.

Don't the sentences look poetic! Contrast them with subordinate clauses and even participle phrases. The superiority of these sentences is apparent. Constructing a Nominative Absolute is rather complicated although it is not always difficult. Absolute indicates independence and Nominative indicates a noun structure. In the above examples, an Active-Continuous Participle Phrase being an Adjective Phrase is describing a Noun Phrase – together they form a longer Noun Phrase. Rules regarding the Active-Continuous Participle Phrase still remain but it is describing another subject instead of the subject or object in the main clause.

Note the Nominative Absolute construction:

<u>**The maids** shivering in fear</u>, <u>**the amok** was threatening them with a chopper</u>.
     (Subject)                   (Main Subject)
  [Noun Phrase] + [Adjective Phrase]
   =    [Independent Noun Phrase]     [Main Clause]

An Adjective Phrase attached to a Noun Phrase forms another Noun Phrase! Also note that the Nominative Absolute cannot exist without the support of a main clause. However, grammatically, the Nominative Absolute does not modify the main clause like an Adverb Phrase nor describe the main clause as an Adjective Phrase. An attempt to call it a Noun Phrase in Apposition fails because it cannot take the place of the subject in the main clause. It is a Noun Phrase related to a main clause only in content or meaning but not in grammar. Therefore, it is ingeniously called an Absolute to show its grammatical independence of the main clause. In context, it relies on the main clause to give it a meaningful existence.

Extreme caution is needed though. Students unable to construct Nominative Absolute structures correctly will write fragmented sentences. Writing Participle Phrases is an alternative though not the best choice. Otherwise, simply write only familiar Nominative Absolutes till you can write them correctly and creatively.

The following sentences will illustrate the problem:

The peasant unwittingly **blaspheming** his god, the priest rebuked him in public. (Correct)

The peasant unwittingly **blaspheming** his god, the priest rebuking him in public. (Wrong)

[There is no full verb in the wrong sentence at all, so it is a fragmented sentence.]

The peasant was unwittingly blaspheming his god, the priest was rebuking him in public. (Wrong)

[The comma separates two Main Clauses when it should be a full stop. There is no Nominative Absolute construction here.]

**Note: The Nominative Absolute may consist of a Noun Phrase and an Adjective Phrase describing the Noun Phrase. The Active-Continuous Participle Phrase is describing the Subject in the Nominative Absolute and not the subject in the**

main clause. **The Nominative Absolute cannot exist without a main clause that it must rely on in a meaningful connection.**

## (b) Converting Clauses into Nominative Absolutes using Active-Continuous Participle Phrase

Any subordinate or main clause containing a subject and an active-continuous action can be converted into a Nominative Absolute using an Active-Continuous Participle Phrase, the subject in the main clause not being the same as the subject in the Nominative Absolute. There must be two different subjects and the two clauses must be related in meaning.

Look at the Adverb Clauses already used earlier as Active-Continuous Participle Phrases and contrast them with the Nominative Absolute constructions. Each main clause needs to be changed to include a different subject.

*While the costumier was dressing up the party-goers*, the hostess was greeting them enthusiastically.
*The costumier **dressing** up the party-goers*, the hostess was greeting them enthusiastically.

*As the vandal was damaging the playground*, two patrolling policemen arrested him.
*The vandal **damaging** the playground*, two patrolling policemen arrested him.

*Although the sentries were guarding the main gate*, firearms were not issued to them.
*The sentries **guarding** the main gate*, firearms were not issued to them.

[Notice that the Adverb Clause sounds more suitable here.]

*Because the pharmacist is dispensing the potent drugs*, the customers felt safe.
*The pharmacist **dispensing** the potent drugs*, the customers felt safe.

Main clauses can also be converted, subordinate clauses transformed into main clauses.

<u>The stallholders are slaughtering live chickens at the stall</u> so that the customers can buy fresh meat.
<u>The stallholders **slaughtering** live chickens at the stall</u>, the customers can buy fresh meat.

<u>The bartender was sipping wine out of the bottles so much</u> that the manager sacked him.
<u>The bartender **sipping** wine out of the bottles too much</u>, the manager sacked him.

As the maestro is satisfied with his understudy, <u>the latter is grinning widely</u>.
<u>The understudy **grinning** widely</u>, the maestro is satisfied with him.

Similarly, Noun Clauses can be converted with additional subjects:

The copywriter was overwhelmed with joy <u>that his advertised copy was obtaining the Best Copywriter Award</u>.
<u>His advertised copy **obtaining** the Best Copywriter Award</u>, the copywriter was overwhelmed with joy.

<u>That the chief administrator will be making her rounds soon</u> keeps the department heads alert in their tasks.
<u>The chief administrator **making** her rounds soon</u>, the department heads are alert in their tasks.

The complainant was apprehensive in <u>what his wife was reporting about the burglary</u>.
<u>His wife **reporting** about the burglary</u>, the complainant was apprehensive.

Now look at Adjective Clauses and their conversions. Only when the Adjective Clause has a different subject can it be converted into a Nominative Absolute. Sometimes we need to rewrite the Adjective Clauses to create a different subject.

The entrepreneur <u>whose new venture was generating huge profits</u> made headline news.

*His new venture **generating** huge profits*, the entrepreneur made headline news.

The hired cruise ship, *which was carrying tourists to the islands*, developed an engine trouble.
*The hired cruise ship **carrying** tourists to the islands*, an engine trouble developed.

The monastery *that drug addicts get help from its charitable service* draws generous donations from the public.
The monastery, *drug addicts **getting** help from its charitable service*, draws generous donations from the public.

Like the Active-Continuous Participle Phrase, the Nominative Absolutes can be derived from many sources, a new subject added if there is a single subject in the sentence, the student having many opportunities of writing this construction in an essay too. However, restraint must be exercised because just a few Nominative Absolutes in a paragraph are enough to fascinate or bewilder the reader or examiner. Do not forget the risk involved. Also, other grammar structures can be equally important for variety.

**Note: Convert clauses into Nominative Absolute constructions only when you are sure of their accuracy but a few short constructions should be enough in a paragraph. Also, not all paragraphs need Nominative Absolutes.**

## (c) Placing Nominative Absolutes using Active-Continuous Participle Phrase in Sentences

It is much easier and safer to place Nominative Absolutes in the beginning of sentences, so make it a habit! However, we can have Nominative Absolutes after the subjects too if you are bold enough to try. Keep them short to avoid making the subject in the main sentence appear isolated in front.

*The ventriloquist, the puppet's lips **moving** actively, is restraining the movement of his own lips to make sound appear coming from the puppet.*
*The President, the contingents **parading** past him, will eye the faces of the proud participants.*
*A patriot, his comrade **betraying** his country, should expose him quickly and decisively.*

The Nominative Absolute must have enclosed commas in any sentence whenever it is placed after the Subject in the Main Clause, indicating that it is independent grammatically of the Main Clause.

A bolder move is to place a Nominative Absolute after the Main Clause at the end of the sentence, a comma separating the Nominative Absolute from the Main Clause to show its independence or absolute nature. This structure is not for the faint hearted because the construction sometimes does not sound right. Not wanting to take this risk of being wrong or wasting time pondering over it in an examination, always be sure when you want to write such a bewildering structure.

*The fugitive escaped into the alley, <u>police constables **chasing** after him</u>.*
*A husband will wait anxiously for the news of the child's gender, <u>the gynaecologist **determining** it with an ultrasound scan</u>.*
*The dental surgeon is drilling the tooth cautiously with his delicate instrument, <u>the patient **anticipating** any sudden pain</u>.*

Mistakes in Nominative Absolute structures being usually very obvious especially with the missing comma or enclosed commas, most errors are made not in grammatical form. Errors are usually made in relating the meaning of the Nominative Absolute to the content of the main clause.

Here are some errors in grammatical form:

*The kitten, the puppy licking its fur lovingly, seems to enjoy the attention.* (Correct)

*The kitten, <u>the puppy **loves** licking its fur</u>, seems to enjoy the attention.* (Wrong)

[The underlined sentence is also a main clause with the full verb "loves" and not a Nominative Absolute.]

*The two rare paintings must have been stolen together, <u>the owner **weeping** terribly for the double loss in one night</u>.* (Correct)

*The two rare paintings must have been stolen together <u>the owner weeping terribly for the double loss in one night</u>.* (Wrong)

[This error is rare for it is obvious a comma is missing before the supposed Nominative Absolute.]

*The toddler, <u>the grandmother **pandering** to her every craving</u>, was spoilt.* (Correct)

*The toddler, <u>the grandmother **pandering** to her every craving</u> had spoilt her.* (Wrong)

[This error, unfortunately, is rather common. The subject in front is most likely forgotten and has no predicate to complete a sentence. Putting a comma after the supposed Nominative Absolute will not save the sentence because "the toddler had spoilt herself" in this case.]

Here are some errors in relating the Nominative Absolute to the content of the main clause:

*The artiste's collection was going to be sold, <u>the auctioneer **raising** his hammer</u>.* (Correct)

*The artiste's collection was finally sold, <u>the auctioneer raising his hammer</u>.* (Wrong)

[The auctioneer must hit the hammer to close the sale and not simply raising it. The construction seems correct but is wrong in content.]

*The engineer has lost the direction to the bridge, <u>a wrong track **leading** him deeper into the jungle</u>.* (Correct)

*The engineer returned safely with the help of the natives, <u>a wrong track leading him deeper into the jungle</u>.* (Wrong)

[The sentence seems to miss a scene when the natives found the engineer.]

*Many people read the horoscope seriously, <u>astrology **revealing** their future</u>.* (Correct)

*Many people believe the stars can tell their future, <u>astrology revealing their future</u>.* (Wrong)

[The Nominative Absolute is redundant because it means the stars are telling their future too.]

*The mistress **hassling** the tycoon for more money*, the media got wind of their affair.  (Correct)

*The mistress **hassling** the tycoon for more money*, she threatened to reveal their affair to the media.  (Poor Usage)

[The second sentence is not wrong but redundant because the subject is doing both actions, so the Nominative Absolute is unnecessary.]

*The mistress, **hassling** the tycoon for more money*, threatened to reveal their affair to the media.  (Correct)

Practice makes perfect!  A slogan that really works especially in constructing Nominative Absolutes, you may become an expert soon if you do not give up trying.

**Note:    Nominative Absolute construction always needs a comma or enclosed commas to separate it from the main clause to show its absolute independence from the main clause.    It can be placed anywhere suitable as long as its meaning is related to the content in the main clause.**

## 1.3.2 Nominative Absolute using Active-Perfect Participle Phrase

### (a) Structure and Function of a Nominative Absolute using Active-Perfect Participle Phrase

Look at some examples of the Nominative Absolute construction using Active-Perfect Participle Phrase:

*Several scouts **having straggled** from the leading group, the scoutmaster halted the hike to wait for them.*
*The weary travellers **having hobbled** to an oasis, their blistered feet finally had a rest.*
*The teenager **having scurried** away from the extortionists, her parents were later informed of the harrowing experience.*

The sentences looking equally poetic contrasted with subordinate clauses or even participle phrases, remember that Absolute means it is an independent phrase and Nominative indicates that it is a Noun Phrase. In the above examples, an Active-Perfect Participle Phrase as an Adjective Phrase is describing a Noun Phrase – together they form a longer Noun Phrase. Rules regarding the Active-Perfect Participle Phrase still remaining, it is describing another subject instead of the subject or object in the main clause.

Note the Nominative Absolute construction:

**The dying tycoon** *having sputtered a few words,* **Death** *took him away*.

    (Subject)                               (Main Subject)
[Noun Phrase] + [Adjective Phrase]
   =   [Independent Noun Phrase]        [Main Clause]

An Adjective Phrase describing a Noun Phrase is another Noun Phrase! Nominative Absolute, only existing with the support of a main clause, does not modify the main clause like an Adverb Phrase nor describe the main clause as an Adjective Phrase. Calling it a Noun Phrase in Apposition fails because it cannot take the place of the subject, a Noun Phrase being related to a main clause only in content or meaning but not in grammar. Therefore, it is ingeniously called an Absolute to show its grammatical independence of the main clause, relying on the main clause in content to give it a meaningful existence.

Does not that paragraph sound familiar? In fact, the arguments for writing a Nominative Absolute using an Active-Perfect Participle Phrase are similar to that of writing a Nominative Absolute using an Active-Continuous Participle Phrase. Note the difference in the Adjective Phrase where the different functions for active-continuous action or active-perfect action apply.

Let us look at some problems in grammatical form:

*The pacifist **having** adamantly **objected** to carrying a real rifle, the platoon commander offered a fake wooden rifle instead.* (Correct)

The pacifist **having** adamantly **objected** to carrying a real rifle, the platoon commander having offered a fake wooden rifle instead.
(Wrong)

[There is no full verb in the wrong sentence at all, so it is a fragmented sentence.]

The pacifist had adamantly objected to carrying a real rifle, the platoon commander had offered a fake wooden rifle instead. (Wrong)

[The comma separates two Main Clauses when it should be a full stop. There is no Nominative Absolute construction here.]

**Note: The Nominative Absolute may consist of a Noun Phrase and an Adjective Phrase describing the Noun Phrase. If the Adjective Phrase is an Active-Perfect Participle Phrase, the rules concerning the completed action of the Active-Perfect Participle Phrase still apply. The Active-Perfect Participle Phrase is describing the Subject in the Nominative Absolute and not the Subject in the main clause. The Nominative Absolute cannot exist without a main clause that it must rely on in a meaningful connection.**

## (b) Converting Clauses into Nominative Absolutes using Active-Perfect Participle Phrase

Any subordinate or main clause containing a subject and an active-perfect action can be converted into a Nominative Absolute using Active-Perfect Participle Phrase, the Subject in the Main Clause not being the same as the Subject in the Nominative Absolute. There must be two different subjects and the two clauses must be related in meaning.

Look at the Adverb Clauses already used earlier as Active-Perfect Participle Phrases and contrast them with the Nominative Absolute constructions. Each main clause needs to be changed to include a different subject.

*After the old retiree had shuffled into his apartment, his heart started palpitating.*
*The old retiree **having shuffled** into his apartment, his heart started palpitating.*

*As the masons have cut the stones, loaded barrels were carrying the stones to the building site.*
*The masons **having cut** the stones, loaded barrels were carrying them to the building site.*

*Though the umpire will have scampered into the field, the game will not start so soon.*
*The umpire **having scampered** into the field, the game will not start so soon.*

*If the child has toddled near the burning stove, the parent will carry him off to safety.*
*The child **having toddled** near the burning stove, the parent will carry him off to safety.*

Main clauses can also be converted when connected with Adverb Clauses. A different subject is included in the Adverb Clauses.

*The teenagers have slunk out of the house, so the guardians are still ignorant.*
*The teenagers **having slunk** out of the house, the guardians are still ignorant.*

*The geishas will have minced onto the stage* so that the businessmen will be entertained.
The geishas **having minced** *onto the stage*, the businessmen will be entertained.

*Her mother had struck a lottery* since a car was bought yesterday.
Her mother **having struck** *a lottery*, a car was bought yesterday.

Similarly, Noun Clauses can be converted with additional subjects and some rephrasing needs to be done too:

The lady tenant was filled with such grief *that she had lost her spouse in an accident*.
The lady tenant **having lost** *her spouse in an accident*, her grief overwhelmed her.

The secretary was expected to deny *that she had complained about her boss to his superior*.
The secretary **having complained** *about her boss to his superior*, a denial from her was expected.

The stragglers were apologetic in *that they had kept the volunteers behind*.
The stragglers **having kept** *the volunteers behind*, an apology was given.

Now look at Adjective Clauses and their conversions.

The stewardess *who had humiliated an airline passenger* was suspended from duty.
The stewardess **having humiliated** *an airline passenger*, her duty was suspended.

The vehicles *which have smuggled drugs into the country* are confiscated by the authorities.
The vehicles **having smuggled** *drugs into the country*, the authorities confiscate the vehicles.

The production operators *whose boss has retrenched them unwillingly* may be rehired later.

*The boss **having retrenched** the production operators unwillingly, they may be rehired later.*

Like the Active-Perfect Participle Phrase, the Nominative Absolute can come from many sources, a new subject added if there is a single subject in the sentence, thus having many opportunities of writing this construction in an essay too. However, restraint must be exercised because just a few Nominative Absolutes in a paragraph are enough to fascinate or bewilder the reader or examiner. Do not forget the risk involved. Also, other grammar structures can be equally important for variety.

**Note: Convert clauses into Nominative Absolute constructions only when you are sure of their accuracy but a few short constructions should be enough in a paragraph. Also, not all paragraphs need Nominative Absolutes.**

## (c) Placing Nominative Absolutes using Active-Perfect Participle Phrase in Sentences

Similarly, it is much easier and safer to place Nominative Absolutes in the beginning of sentences, so make it a habit! However, we can have Nominative Absolutes after the subjects too if you are bold enough to try. Keep them short to avoid making the subject in the main sentence appear isolated in front. However, since the active-perfect action is quite emphatic, a Nominative Absolute longer than the main sentence may work too.

*The principal, the culprit **having blurted** the truth, will inform his parents of the misdeed.*
*The professor, a few law students **having failed** to impress him, decided to give them a second chance.*
*The soprano, her performance **having wooed** the audience, sang an encore.*

The Nominative Absolute must have enclosed commas in any sentence whenever it is placed after the Subject in the Main Clause, showing its absolute independence grammatically of the Main Clause.

A bolder move being to place a Nominative Absolute after the Main Clause at the end of the sentence, remember there must always be a comma separating the Nominative Absolute from the Main Clause to show its independence or absolute nature.  This structure is not for the faint hearted, its construction sometimes sounding unusual.  You do not want to take this risk of being wrong or waste time pondering over it in an examination.  So always be sure when you want to write such a bewildering structure.

*One of the chess competitors refused to continue the match, <u>spectators **having distracted** his concentration by their whisperings.</u>*
*The client finally purchased the condominium apartment, <u>his wife **having scrutinized**  the new dwelling closely</u>.*
*An admirer of the pretty model was battered by a thug, <u>the former's eyes **having ogled** at the latter's girlfriend</u>.*

Mistakes in Nominative Absolute structures being usually very obvious without the comma or enclosed commas, most errors are made not in grammatical form.  Errors are usually made in relating the meaning of the Nominative Absolute to the content of the Main Clause.

Here are some errors in grammatical form:

*The penitent, <u>the crime **having wasted** several years of his life in prison</u>, can return to society without a criminal record if he remains clean.*  (Correct)

*The penitent, <u>the crime **has wasted** several years of his life in prison</u>, can return to society without a criminal record if he remains clean.*   (Wrong)

[The underlined sentence is also a main clause with the full verb "has wasted" and not a Nominative Absolute.]

*The children suspected Grandfather needed a pair of spectacles**,** <u>the old librarian **having squinted** his eyes</u>.*    (Correct)

*The children suspected Grandfather needed a pair of spectacles <u>the old librarian **having squinted** his eyes</u>.*   (Wrong)

[This error is rare for it is obvious a comma is missing before the supposed Nominative Absolute.]

*Many journalists have requested an admission to the crowded news conference, <u>a medical scientist **having claimed** to have found a cure for AIDS</u>.* (Correct)

*Many journalists, <u>a medical scientist **having claimed** to have found a cure for AIDS attracts</u> them.* (Wrong)

[This error, unfortunately, is rather common. The subject in front is most likely forgotten and has no predicate to complete a sentence. Putting a comma after the supposed Nominative Absolute will not save the sentence.]

Here are some errors in relating the Nominative Absolute to the content of the Main Clause:

*The novice hunters started shooting aimlessly, <u>a tiger **having emerged** at a far distance</u>.* (Correct)

*The novice hunters started shooting aimlessly, <u>a tiger **having died** from a gunshot wound</u>.* (Wrong)

[The novice hunters started shooting but the tiger could not have died before that. The construction seems correct but is wrong in content.]

*Representatives from different countries were able to communicate with one another, <u>the assigned linguists **having translated** their intentions effectively</u>.* (Correct)

*Representatives from different countries were attending the trade conference, <u>the assigned linguists **having translated** their intentions effectively</u>.* (Wrong)

[The Nominative Absolute construction appears correct grammatically but it does not link well with the content in the main clause.]

*The corrupt army general quickly stepped in to fence off the area, <u>a prospector **having dug** up gold there</u>.* (Correct)

*The corrupt army general quickly stepped in to fence off the area, a prospector having dug up gold there and <u>having become a multi-millionaire</u>.* (Wrong)

[It would take some time for the prospector to become a multi-millionaire since the army had fenced off the area.]

After much practice, you may find it harder to make mistakes in constructing Nominative Absolutes – that is the ultimate goal!

**Note:　　Nominative Absolute construction always needs a comma or enclosed commas to separate it from the main clause to show its absolute independence from the main clause.　　It can be placed anywhere suitable as long as its meaning is related to the content in the main clause.**

## 1.3.3 Nominative Absolute using Adjective

### (a) Structure and Function of a Nominative Absolute using Adjective

Look at some examples of the Nominative Absolute construction using Adjective, Adjectives or Adjective Phrase with Adverb modifier:

*His hair fully **grey**, the police sergeant draws respect from his young peers.*
*The design **imaginative**, the artist was applauded for his creativity.*
*Children **active** and **noisy**, the grandparents find their home alive once more.*

An Adjective Phrase "fully grey" is formed by adding an Adverb or Adverb Phrase to modify an Adjective. A Nominative Absolute using only one Adjective appears short and sometimes awkward as it does not seem to fit well with the rest of the sentence. However, assuming it is correct structurally, a Nominative Absolute should sound aesthetic when presented in a sentence. Being already independent grammatically of the main clause, it is too risky to sound bad. So adding one Adverb modifier or one more Adjective can make it sound better.

Note the Nominative Absolute construction:

**Her insight** remarkably **perceptive**,     the columnist   is often praised.

(Subject)                                      (Main Subject)
[Noun Phrase] + [Adjective Phrase]
= [Independent Noun Phrase]                    [Main Clause]

Few mistakes are possible because normally a full verb with action and time elements is hardly seen in the construction

**Note:    The Nominative Absolute using Adjective, Adjectives or Adjective Phrase with Adverb modifier is a construction simpler than other types of Nominative Absolute though it may be difficult to sound nice with just one Adjective.**

## (b) Converting Clauses into Nominative Absolutes using Adjective

As long as there is an Adjective in any subordinate or main clause, the clause can be converted into a Nominative Absolute using Adjective. We shall only look at some examples here.

Adverb Clauses are converted:

*As the farmer appears fussy and rude*, the hikers moved on without getting his help.
*The farmer **fussy** and **rude***, the hikers moved on without getting his help.

*Since the old tractor is troublesome*, a bull should do the job.
*The old tractor **troublesome***, a bull should do the job.

*Although stewardesses are pretty and courteous*, skilful handling of passengers is a more essential requirement.
*Stewardesses **pretty** and **courteous***, skilful handling of passengers is a more essential requirement.

Adjective Clauses are converted:

*Swimmers and sun tanners who find the weather balmy crowd the beach.*
*The weather **balmy***, swimmers and sun tanners crowd the beach.

Marine police are combing the island for the pirates *that were brutal and dangerous*.
*The pirates **brutal** and **dangerous**,* marine police are combing the island.

The bankrupt, *whose relatives regard as irresponsible and luckless in business*, is being avoided.
*The bankrupt **irresponsible** and **luckless** in business*, relatives are avoiding him.

Main Clauses are converted:

*The terrorists*, whose life might be sacrificed, *were feeling scared and desperate*.
*The terrorists **scared** and **desperate***, their life might be sacrificed.

*The washing machine is less tedious and timesaving* although some housewives still regard hand washing as thorough and cleaner.
*The washing machine less **tedious** and **timesaving***, some housewives still regard hand washing as thorough and cleaner.

*The winners are exuberant* that each will be given a model contract in a reputable agency.
*The winners **exuberant***, each will be given a model contract in a reputable agency.

Noun Clauses are converted:

*That the bank teller was reckless and negligent* allowed the robbers to escape.
*The bank teller **reckless** and **negligent***, the robbers were allowed to escape.

The orphanage matron is assured *that the lost child is safe and sound*.
*The lost child **safe** and **sound***, the orphanage matron is assured.

The fact *that the cause is feasible and beneficial to society* draws much support from donors.
*The cause **feasible** and **beneficial** to society*, much support is drawn from donors.

It is noted from some examples that prepositional phrases can be used as Adverb Phrases to modify an Adjective.

**Note:     Practically any Adjective in any subordinate or main clause can be used to construct a Nominative Absolute with the related subject.**

## (c)     Placing Nominative Absolutes using Adjective in Sentences

Nominative Absolutes using Adjective usually do not have any full verb with action and time elements in the construction, thus there being fewer errors in placing them in sentences.  The locations are in the usual places – in the beginning of the sentence, right after the subject in the sentence and at the end of the sentence.

> *The sick writer, <u>his face **pale** and **haggard**</u>, was penning a poem about death.*
> *<u>Her speech **eloquent**</u>, the negotiator caught the attention of both parties.*
> *The old sculptor uttered a few words, <u>his panting **shallow**</u>, <u>his eyes **blurry**</u> and <u>his message **short** and **vague**</u>.*

Where a full verb with action and time factors is found in the construction, the necessary cautions for proper content or sequence linkage must be observed.

> <u>*The parents **furious** with their daughter because she **came** home late one night*</u>, *a curfew was enforced.*
> <u>*Beer drinkers **contentious** in their behaviour as they **are drinking**</u>, other customers may stay clear of the coffee shop.*
> <u>*The housewives **calculative** and **demanding** in what they **have perceived** to be lower quality goods*</u>, *bazaar stallholders should expect haggling over the prices.*

You have practised action and time factors of tenses extensively in the earlier part of the course.

**Note:     Most Nominative Absolutes using Adjective do not have a full verb with action and time factors included unless a subordinate clause is added, placing the Nominative Absolute being easier in this case.**

## 1.3.4 Combination of Nominative Absolutes

Combining Nominative Absolutes in a sentence tending to produce a rather lengthy sentence, Nominative Absolute constructions should be kept as short as possible. There are no fixed locations for any types of Nominative Absolute, the aesthetic presentation being more significant. Here are some examples:

*Stiff legs **having plodded** up the stairs*, his eyes **blurry** *from a long drive* and ***scrutinizing*** *each door number*, the trader was in a dimly lit motel, seeking a warm shelter on that cold rainy night.

*Rugged hands **having crumbled** the crispy bread*, *the retiree **dropping** the crumbs into a fish tank*, the printing factory having occupied most of his life entered his mind, *his working days **busy** and **fruitful***.

*A few crew members **scurrying** after the young stowaways*, *a child's whimpering **having revealed** the hideout*, the captain announced for their immediate capture, *a father himself **sympathetic** with their plight and more **worried** for their safety*.

*The soccer fans **aflame** and **belligerent***, *riot police **having separated** the opposing gangs*, windows of stores were shattered as they marched, *stationary vehicles **burning** in their path*.

*Pirates **having commandeered** a container ship*, *the incident **newsworthy***, a media helicopter was monitoring its movement, *navy boats **nipping** towards the location*.

Putting a few Nominative Absolutes together in a sentence takes some time. Therefore, it is essential to practise writing them before any essay examination. Use whatever you can remember and write easily without wasting precious time, this advice being very important for examination students. However, two or three Nominative Absolutes in a sentence are impressive enough.

**Note: Combining Nominative Absolutes in a sentence is impressive. However, it must be done within a short time, only writing a construction that is familiar or can be done easily.**

@@@@@@@@@@@@@@@@@@@@@@@@@@@@@@@@

> Refer to Self-Practice 1.3 and Assignments 5 & 6 to complete the exercises there before you continue with the notes here.

@@@@@@@@@@@@@@@@@@@@@@@@@@@@@@@@

# SELF-PRACTICE 1.3

(These Exercises Should Be Done Before The Assignments. Do Not Submit Them As Answers Are Provided At The End.)

EXERCISE 1: POETIC SENTENCES ARE EVEN MORE AMAZING!

**Combine the sentences by replacing the sentence or clause with an <u>underlined word</u> with a Nominative Absolute using an Active-Continuous Participle Phrase or simply an Active-Continuous Participle Phrase if the subject does both actions without changing the content.** The phrase can be located in any part of the sentence if appropriate.

Examples:

a.   Students are <u>gallivanting</u> in the nearby shopping malls in school uniform. The principal advises them to change before going shopping.
*Answer:   a.   <u>Students **gallivanting** in the nearby shopping malls in school uniform</u>, the principal advises them to change before going shopping.*

b.   As the soccer fans were <u>jostling</u> one another to enter the auditorium, a stampede seemed imminent.
*Answer:   b.   <u>The soccer fans **jostling** one another to enter the auditorium</u>, a stampede seemed imminent.*

c.   The hawkers appeared worried while the hygiene officers were <u>inspecting</u> their stalls.
*Answer: c. The hawkers appeared worried, <u>the hygiene officers **inspecting** their stalls</u>.*

d.   The ruling party <u>rebutted</u> the points raised effectively.  The opposition members remained silent throughout the rest of the seating in Parliament.
*Answer: d. The opposition members, <u>the ruling party **rebutting** the points raised effectively</u>, remained silent throughout the rest of the seating in Parliament.*

e.   The molester was <u>fondling</u> a young girl at the lift.  He fled when she suddenly shrieked for help.
*Answer:   e.   The molester, <u>**fondling** a young girl at the lift</u>, fled when she suddenly shrieked for help.*

[The underlined phrase is a Participle Phrase and not a Nominative Absolute as the subject does both actions.]

WRITE OUT YOUR ANSWERS ON ANY A4 SIZE SINGLE-LINED PAPERS.

1. The adventurous canoeists were <u>meandering</u> along the river. They were wending through boulders and other boats.
2. The frantic father was <u>pacing</u> to and fro outside the surgery theatre. The son was yelling in pain as a needle was sewing up the slit.
3. The veteran soldier is narrating his war experiences. His scars <u>reveal</u> the truth of his stories.
4. A drug addict was <u>reeling</u> onto the busy street. A Good Samaritan attempted to catch hold of him.
5. The extremely myopic professor was waddling clumsily along the corridor. He <u>bumped</u> into a few students.
6. The sewing machine pricked the needle through her finger. The seamstress was <u>nipping</u> the pieces of cloth in place.
7. The reckless youth <u>lacerated</u> the cardboard into two pieces although a pair of scissors was on the table.
8. The creaky bus was <u>careening</u> expertly down the narrow mountain road. The passengers were flabbergasted.
9. The judge is <u>mulling</u> a death sentence for the convicted killer. He is concerned about the mitigating factor.
10. The aircraft carrier loomed before the visitors as the transport craft was <u>manoeuvring</u> nearer to its hull.
11. The vagrants <u>settled</u> along the seaside. The fishermen were suspicious of them.
12. The dolphins are chirping cheerfully in the waves. Killer sharks may be <u>lurking</u> dangerously close by.
13. The garbage bin is <u>reeking</u> of a concoction of decaying foods. Residents can only avoid the stench by holding their breath for a while.
14. Couples <u>saunter</u> along the dimly lit beach. Robbers sometimes prey on these unsuspecting lovebirds especially in isolated areas.
15. The abusive boyfriend was <u>smacking</u> the daughter's face. The mother cowardly defended his action as a form of discipline for the rebellious brat.
16. The motorists are <u>glowering</u> at each other for a trivial fault. Road rage usually starts with such discourteous behaviour.
17. The negotiator was <u>interposing</u> on certain occasions. He was trying to close the sale as the intermediary between the two businessmen.
18. Her peers were <u>scoffing</u> at her failed attempt to get a promotion. They noticed her dining with the boss the night before.

19.   The husband's stomach was <u>growling</u> in despair and hunger.  The wife refused to start dinner unless the guests arrived.
20.   The media tycoon is <u>impugning</u> the declaration by the minister to eradicate poverty.  The former asserts that the minister's family is the richest in the country.
21.   Computers are <u>sprouting</u> up all over the countryside.  Wireless connection is making this possible.
22.   Audio visual aids <u>stimulate</u> the students to sense their lessons.  They remember them better even for a long period of time.
23.   Monthly magazines <u>bombard</u> consumers with the latest information.  Advertisements are abundant in these magazines to capture their specific markets.
24.   Profit maximization is overcoming business ethics as the sole motivation for survival in a competitive world.  Legal suits <u>arise</u> from disagreements in business transactions.
25.   Morality is <u>pricking</u> the conscience of donors who are reluctantly withholding contributions to charitable organizations because of a few black sheep.


### EXERCISE 2: GETTING IT RIGHT WITH TWO SUBJECTS?

**Circle the number** on the left if the sentence is **grammatically or factually wrong**. Sometimes it can be difficult to determine which words are wrong, so underline all the disagreeable actions or indicators if you can.

1.   The orphans' saliva dribbling from their mouths, were staring at the durian cakes on the table.
2.   The armed burglar coercing the teenager to unlock the drawer, a penknife sticking to his neck.
3.   The human resource officer vetting applicants for the highly technological post, only one seems qualified in terms of experience.
4.   Pretty high-class ladies snubbing the poorly dressed gentlemen in the discotheque, the dancing floor having more ladies than men.
5.   Air force personnel were scurrying towards their posts, the base alarm sounding vigorously.
6.   The heiress' heart yearning for an honest caring man, was spurning all the handsome suitors.
7.   The ferocious beast intimidating the fort dwellers, hunters stalking the elusive animal, the natives worshipping it as a manifestation of their god.

8. Inspiring a Christmas spirit, shoppers are mesmerized by the numerous gift items available.
9. Impelling the soldiers to donate blood, the press reported the unfair tactic.
10. Allegations of bribery darting at the mayor, corruption may raise its ugly head once again in the city.
11. The local community is ostracizing the cult group living in the remote outskirt of town, supplies are normally delivered to them by a few retail shops.
12. An eccentric banker rarely socializing with his staff or clients, reading odd books luring him to the old library each evening.
13. Donkeys humping packs of mineral rocks, the old miners were plodding towards the exit.
14. Fishermen, trawlers hauling in the nets, are always confident of an abundant supply of fish.
15. Recuperating from a depression, a schedule of several film roles aided in the actor's recovery.


EXERCISE 3: ADJECTIVES ARE IMPRESSIVE!

**Form a Nominative Absolute using Adjective with the given underlined Adjective in each sentence, any suitable location being acceptable.**

Examples:

a. The social worker, who was empathic and diligent, transported the homeless beggar to a welfare home.
*Answer: a. The social worker **empathic** and **diligent**, the homeless beggar was transported to a welfare home.*


b. Two cyclists were rowdy and ready for a brawl when a policeman halted their childish squabble.
*Answer: b. A policeman, two cyclists **rowdy** and **ready** for a brawl, halted their childish squabble.*

c. His head was bloody and his eyes were extremely red yet the motorist did not realized he was badly injured.
*Answer: c. The motorist did not realize he was badly injured, his head **bloody** and his eyes extremely **red**.*

WRITE OUT YOUR ANSWERS ON ANY A4 SIZE SINGLE-LINED PAPERS.

1. As the famous painter is <u>unassuming</u> and <u>sociable</u>, the apprentices are enjoying his capable instruction.
2. The girl is <u>squeamish</u> about watching a horror movie so that her date has to endure a boring romantic movie.
3. The janitor, whose punctuality is <u>well known</u>, opens up the school early in the morning.
4. The foreman knows how to motivate the <u>simple</u> and <u>vulgar</u> labourers.
5. A country's defence relies on its armed forces where fighting men are <u>loyal</u> and <u>brave</u>.
6. The young cadet was standing proudly in his <u>smart</u> and <u>clean</u> uniform.
7. Military law is stern and merciless where cowards may be shot in battle.
8. A regular drug user appears <u>gaunt</u> and <u>haggard</u> and is easily spotted.
9. The journalist did not envisage that he would be arrested since the news report was <u>innocuous</u> about the life of a retired political leader.
10. Bugging of a political opponent's office is <u>intrusive</u>, <u>illegal</u> and <u>unforgivable</u> in the public's eyes, a powerful president had to step down from office.
11. The host, whose clothes are <u>flamboyant</u> and hair is <u>wiry</u> and <u>brown</u>, stalks onto the stage.
12. The condemned criminal slouches along the corridor with a <u>solemn</u> face while each step is <u>slow</u> and <u>weak</u> as though he may collapse.
13. As the morning sky is <u>bright</u> and <u>clear</u>, air is <u>fresh</u> and birds are <u>melodious</u>, the day seems good for a jog in the park.
14. Expecting the culprit to return, the undercover detective lurked at the void deck, his hunch wild as usual, his prediction ludicrous as no evidence would support his claim.
15. Even though the task is <u>arduous</u> and <u>daunting</u>, the police commissioner's resolve is <u>ardent</u> as the government is backing him and so he intends to eradicate corruption within the force soon.

@@@@@@@@@@@@@@@@@@@@@@@@@@@@@@@@@

Check your answers at the end. Refer to Assignment 5 and complete the exercises there for submission before you continue with the next exercises here.

@@@@@@@@@@@@@@@@@@@@@@@@@@@@@@@@@

EXERCISE 4: MORE POETIC SENTENCES!

**Combine the sentences by replacing the sentence or clause with an <u>underlined word</u> with a Nominative Absolute using Active-Perfect Participle Phrase or simply an Active-Perfect Participle Phrase if the subject does both actions without changing the content.** The phrase can be located in any part of the sentence if appropriate. Write the answers on A4 size single-lined papers.

Examples:

a.  The cheerleaders <u>pranced</u> into the field. The rugby players marched in.
*Answer: a. <u>The cheerleaders **having pranced** into the field</u>, the rugby players marched in.*

b.  The loan shark <u>crinkled</u> the paper. The list of the man's debts vanished in the rubbish chute.
*Answer: b. The list of the man's debts, <u>the loan shark **having crinkled** the paper</u>, vanished in the rubbish chute.*

c.  The client revealed his childhood miseries after the psychiatrist had <u>hypnotized</u> him.
*Answer: c. The client revealed his childhood miseries, <u>the psychiatrist **having hypnotized** him</u>.*

d.  The supposed alibi <u>contradicted</u> the suspect's statement. He put his friend at the scene of the crime instead.
*Answer: d. The supposed alibi, **having contradicted** <u>the suspect's statement</u>, put his friend at the scene of the crime instead.*

[The underlined phrase is a Participle Phrase and not a Nominative Absolute as the subject does both actions.]

WRITE OUT YOUR ANSWERS ON ANY A4 SIZE SINGLE-LINED PAPERS.

1.  The celebrity <u>slunk</u> out of the airport. The fans were disappointed.
2.  Rescue ships were combing the area where the passenger liner sank. Most of the survivors <u>swam</u> to an island.
3.  The flood <u>swept</u> the bridge away so the villagers were stranded.
4.  Since the explorers had <u>trudged</u> into the unknown city, several of the porters mysteriously disappeared.

5. The villain <u>abducts</u> a pretty woman. He sets up a trap to ambush the hero.
6. The bodyguard <u>swivelled</u> round to face the stalker. His fiery eyes were glaring at the stubborn fan.
7. The disciple <u>exorcized</u> the demon. The child scampered towards the happy parents.
8. The lamp <u>glimmered</u> in the haunted house. The curious teenagers plodded into the deserted dwelling place.
9. The wound on the soldier's foot <u>festered</u>. The medic immediately disinfected it with potassium permanganate.
10. If the gravy <u>coagulates</u> in the bottom of the pan, it has to be heated and stirred.
11. The Health Science Authority <u>assays</u> the new drugs as being safe before patients are allowed to use them.
12. The garbage collectors <u>guffawed</u> for a moment before they pulled their fellow worker out of the garbage in the truck.
13. Public accountants <u>audit</u> companies' final accounts because they represent independent parties without investments in those companies.
14. Many male customers are lured to the motor show by scantily clad models who have <u>beguiled</u> them.
15. The secretary <u>concocted</u> an excuse for the manager. His wife could not drag him out of the office that day.
16. The computer hobbyist <u>contrived</u> a bulky mixture of equipments to cool down his computer. The central processing unit was overclocked to its highest level.
17. The hairstylist <u>snipped</u> away the sideburns. The lad was devastated by his new look in the mirror.
18. The retirees <u>accumulate</u> wealth in their younger days. They surmise a life of daily entertainment in their older days.
19. The police evacuated the building and cordoned the area. The demolition team <u>embedded</u> explosives in strategic locations.
20. Both parties <u>stipulated</u> the terms for the franchise. The lawyers ensured that the documents were properly signed and sealed.
21. The ancient drama <u>depicted</u> a crowning ceremony. Many historians thought a new king did come to the throne.
22. Serial numbers <u>authenticate</u> famous paintings. Buyers and sellers of art transact their business easily this way.
23. A landlord adversely <u>possessed</u> a piece of his neighbour's land. That piece of property would be his after twenty-one years under the old law in Singapore.

24. The hijackers <u>commandeered</u> an Italian ship. The police had to negotiate with them to release the hostages.
25. The teacher <u>confiscated</u> the student's mobile phone. A muffled weeping was heard throughout the lesson.


<u>EXERCISE 5</u>: GETTING IT RIGHT WITH TWO SUBJECTS AGAIN?

**Circle the number** on the left if the sentence is **grammatically or factually wrong**. Sometimes it can be difficult to determine which words are wrong, so underline all the disagreeable actions or indicators if you can.

1. Having perforated the plastic cover of the bottle, the fish can breathe easily.
2. The research analysts having forecast healthy growth in the economy next year, investors are bullish or positive that share prices will rise.
3. Manicurists having emerged only recently in the local market, a growing clientele.
4. Having averted a medical crisis in the use of antibiotics, the bird flu is the next hurdle.
5. Arabian countries having monopolized the oil market, oil price tending to move upwards.
6. Neighbouring countries have antagonized one another, trading with one another keeps them together.
7. Research and development engineers having miniaturized storage disks, portable equipments can now carry more memory.
8. Abductors having beheaded their hostages, terrorists having exploded bombs mindlessly to kill innocent people, both having no sense of morality.
9. Ethnic conflicts having arisen because of a few racist thugs on either side, perpetuators must be brought to justice quickly before an escalation.
10. Having drowsed through the show, a bad review of the film will prevail in the critic's column.
11. The rebels, their leader having mustered reinforcements from the countryside, advancing towards the capital to overthrow the government and its army.
12. Her lips having quivered initially, the mother knew she was hesitating to tell the truth.
13. The surgeon, the scalpel having slit open the wound, having tweaked the bullet from its wedged location.
14. The novice swimmer, his head having submerged in the water, panicked when he tried to breathe.

15.   The salesman had plonked the soda can onto the desk, the spilt liquid had wetted a few invoices.


EXERCISE 6: COMBINING POETIC SENTENCES FOR MORE POWER!

**Convert the underlined clauses or sentences into Nominative Absolutes and combine them with the remaining main clause to form a single sentence.**

Example:

a.   His eyes are bulging as if they are popping out.   His face is sallow and shiny with sweat.   The physician has confirmed a high fever.   The patient is admitted into the hospital for observation.
Answer: a. *Eyes **bulging** as if they are popping out, face **sallow** and **shiny** with sweat, the physician **having confirmed** a high fever, the patient is admitted into the hospital for observation.*

b.   Since her current charitable actions are bizarre for the stingy heiress has rejected all past requests for donations, people wonder what changed her life recently as reporters are seeking an interview with the eccentric woman.
Answer: b. *Her current charitable actions **bizarre**, the stingy heiress **having rejected** all past requests for donations, people wonder what changed her life recently, reporters **seeking** an interview with the eccentric woman.*


WRITE OUT YOUR ANSWERS ON ANY A4 SIZE SINGLE-LINED PAPERS.

1.   As she has souvenirs aplenty in the glass cabinets and is a keen traveller who has traversed the American continent and European countries, she is now eyeing either Africa or China in which a decision is still lingering in her mind.

2.   His reaction was anomalous as the board had dismissed him as the school principal.   The veteran educator calmly strode out of the conference room while a few members were approaching him and bidding him farewell.

3.   The comrades were waving hands frantically as the ship had steered away from the dock.   The old communist leader, whose eyes were bleary, shook his right fist in the air.

4. <u>Though the hot desert is hazardous to novice explorers, archaeologists have dug out historical ruins in the inhospitable land</u>. A romantic adventure awaits the foolhardy or an astute researcher <u>while the warm sand is luring either to death or life in the past</u>.

5. <u>A new fantasy story is invigorating to the mind</u>. <u>Special effects have mesmerized television viewers at home in a short preview</u>. <u>The movie spans two hours</u>. Cinemagoers are eagerly booking advance tickets.

6. <u>Resentment of stronger opponents is consuming her life</u> so that the tennis player trains for hours. <u>The coach is supportive but wary</u> <u>because heat exhaustion has landed her in hospital once</u>.

7. <u>Her heart was throbbing</u> <u>as her leering had attracted the handsome man's attention</u> but she wondered if he would be approaching her <u>even though it was an uncertain and elusive wish</u>.

8. <u>When war correspondents are responsible and truthful</u>, <u>strict censorship has succumbed to such noble and brave reporters</u> <u>since a story in the frontline is risking their life</u> - the camera and pen are their primary weapons.

9. <u>While hands were shivering a little and were icy cold</u>, <u>eyes had shut</u> and his mind was slipping away.

10. <u>A voice had summoned him for dinner.</u> The junior left the playground. <u>His sandals were shuffling towards home</u> <u>but his eyes were misty as he left his friends behind</u>.

@@@@@@@@@@@@@@@@@@@@@@@@@@@@@@

Check your answers at the end. Refer to Assignment 6 and complete the exercises there for submission before you continue with the next segment of notes.

@@@@@@@@@@@@@@@@@@@@@@@@@@@@@@

# Answers for Self-Practice 1.3

## EXERCISE 1

If your alternative answer sounds incorrect because you have placed your phrase in a different location, confirm it with your tutor.

1. The adventurous canoeists, **meandering** along the river, were wending through boulders and other boats.
2. The frantic father **pacing** to and fro outside the surgery theatre, the son was yelling in pain as a needle was sewing up the slit.
3. The veteran soldier is narrating his war experiences, his scars **revealing** the truth of his stories.
4. A Good Samaritan, a drug addict **reeling** onto the busy street, attempted to catch hold of him.
5. The extremely myopic professor was waddling clumsily along the corridor, **bumping** into a few students.
6. The sewing machine, the seamstress **nipping** the pieces of cloth in place, pricked the needle through her finger.
7. The reckless youth **lacerating** the cardboard into two pieces, a pair of scissors was on the table.
8. The creaky bus **careening** expertly down the narrow mountain road, the passengers were flabbergasted.
9. The judge, **mulling** a death sentence for the convicted killer, is concerned about the mitigating factor.
10. The aircraft carrier loomed before the visitors, the transport craft **manoeuvring** nearer to its hull.
11. The vagrants **settling** along the seaside, the fishermen were suspicious of them.
12. The dolphins chirping cheerfully in the waves, killer sharks may be **lurking** dangerously close by.
13. The garbage bin **reeking** of a concoction of decaying foods, residents can only avoid the stench by holding their breath for a while.
14. Robbers, couples **sauntering** along the dimly lit beach, sometimes prey on these unsuspecting lovebirds especially in isolated areas.
15. The abusive boyfriend **smacking** the daughter's face, the mother cowardly defended his action as a form of discipline for the rebellious brat.
16. The motorists **glowering** at each other for a trivial fault, road rage usually starts with such discourteous behaviour.
17. The negotiator, **interposing** on certain occasions, was trying to close the sale as the intermediary between the two businessmen.

18. Her peers, **scoffing** at her failed attempt to get a promotion, noticed her dining with the boss the night before.
19. The husband's stomach **growling** in despair and hunger, the wife refused to start dinner unless the guests arrived.
20. The media tycoon, **impugning** the declaration by the minister to eradicate poverty, asserts that the minister's family is the richest in the country.
21. Computers **sprouting** up all over the countryside, wireless connection is making this possible.
22. Audio visual aids **stimulating** the students to sense their lessons, they remember them better even for a long period of time.
23. Advertisements, monthly magazines **bombarding** consumers with the latest information, are abundant in these magazines to capture their specific markets.
24. Profit maximization, legal suits **arising** from disagreements in business transactions, is overcoming business ethics as the sole motivation for survival in a competitive world.
25. Donors, morality **pricking** their conscience, are reluctantly withholding contributions to charitable organizations because of a few black sheep.


# EXERCISE 2

1. **Their saliva** dribbling from their mouths, **the orphans** were staring at the durian cakes on the table.
2. The armed burglar **was coercing** the teenager to unlock the drawer, a penknife sticking to his neck.
3. The sentence is correct.
4. Pretty high-class ladies **are snubbing** the poorly dressed gentlemen in the discotheque, the dancing floor having more ladies than men.
5. The sentence is correct.
6. **Her heart** yearning for an honest caring man, **the heiress** was spurning all the handsome suitors.
7. The ferocious beast **was intimidating** the fort dwellers, hunters stalking the elusive animal, the natives worshipping it as a manifestation of their god.
8. **Retailers inspiring customers with a Christmas spirit**, shoppers are mesmerized by the numerous gift items available.
9. **Superiors impelling** the soldiers to donate blood, the press reported the unfair tactic.
10. The sentence is correct.
11. The local community **ostracizing** the cult group living in the remote outskirt of town, supplies are normally delivered to them by a few retail shops.

12. An eccentric banker rarely socializing with his staff or clients, reading odd books **lures** him to the old library each evening.
13. The sentence is correct.
14. The sentence is correct.
15. **The actor recuperating** from a depression, a schedule of several film roles aided in the actor's recovery.


EXERCISE 3

1. The famous painter **unassuming and sociable**, the apprentices are enjoying his capable instruction.
2. The girl **squeamish** about watching a horror movie, her date has to endure a boring romantic movie.
3. The janitor, his punctuality **well-known**, opens up the school early in the morning.
4. The foreman, the labourers **simple and vulgar**, knows how to motivate them.
5. A country's defence relies on its armed forces, fighting men **loyal and brave**.
6. The young cadet was standing proudly, his uniform **smart and clean**.
7. Military law **stern and merciless**, cowards may be shot in battle.
8. His appearance **gaunt and haggard**, a regular drug user is easily spotted.
9. The journalist did not envisage that he would be arrested, the news report **innocuous** about the life of a retired political leader.
10. Bugging of a political opponent's office **intrusive, illegal and unforgivable** in the public's eyes, a powerful president had to step down from office.
11. Clothes **flamboyant**, hair **wiry and brown**, the host stalks onto the stage.
12. The condemned criminal slouches along the corridor, face **solemn**, each step **slow and weak** as though he may collapse.
13. The morning sky **bright and clear**, air **fresh**, birds **melodious**, the day seems good for a jog in the park.
14. Expecting the culprit to return, the undercover detective lurked at the void deck, his hunch **wild** as usual, his prediction **ludicrous** as no evidence would support his claim.
15. The task **arduous and daunting**, his resolve **ardent** as the government is backing him, the police commissioner intends to eradicate corruption within the force soon.

EXERCISE 4

1. The celebrity **having slunk** out of the airport, the fans were disappointed.
2. Rescue ships were combing the area where the passenger liner sank, most of the survivors **having swum** to an island.
3. The villagers, the flood **having swept** the bridge away, were stranded.
4. The explorers **having trudged** into the unknown city, several of the porters mysteriously disappeared.
5. The villain, **having abducted** a pretty woman, sets up a trap to ambush the hero.
6. The bodyguard **having swivelled** round to face the stalker, his fiery eyes were glaring at the stubborn fan.
7. The child, the disciple **having exorcized** the demon, scampered towards the happy parents.
8. The lamp **having glimmered** in the haunted house, the curious teenagers plodded into the deserted dwelling place.
9. The medic, the wound on the soldier's foot **having festered**, immediately disinfected it with potassium permanganate.
10. The gravy, **having coagulated** in the bottom of the pan, has to be heated and stirred.
11. The Health Science Authority **having assayed** the new drugs as being safe, patients are allowed to use them.
12. The garbage collectors, **having guffawed** for a moment, pulled their fellow worker out of the garbage in the truck.
13. Public accountants, **having audited** companies' final accounts, represent independent parties without investments in those companies.
14. Many male customers are lured to the motor show, scantily clad models **having beguiled** them.
15. The secretary **having concocted** an excuse for the manager, his wife could not drag him out of the office that day.
16. The computer hobbyist **having contrived** a bulky mixture of cooling equipments to cool down his computer, the central processing unit was overclocked to its highest level.
17. The lad, the hairstylist **having snipped** away the sideburns, was devastated by his new look in the mirror.
18. The retirees, **having accumulated** wealth in their younger days, surmise a life of daily entertainment in their older days.
19. The police evacuated the building and cordoned the area, the demolition team **having embedded** explosives in strategic locations.
20. Both parties **having stipulated** the terms for the franchise, the lawyers ensured that the documents were properly signed and sealed.

21. Many historians, <u>the ancient drama **having depicted** a crowning ceremony</u>, thought a new king did come to the throne.
22. <u>Serial numbers **having authenticated** famous paintings</u>, buyers and sellers of art transact their business easily this way.
23. <u>A landlord **having** adversely **possessed** a piece of his neighbour's land</u>, that piece of property would be his after twenty-one years under the old law in Singapore.
24. The police, <u>the hijackers **having commandeered** an Italian ship</u>, had to negotiate with them to release the hostages.
25. <u>The teacher **having confiscated** the student's mobile phone</u>, a muffled weeping was heard throughout the lesson.


# EXERCISE 5

1. **The owner having perforated** the plastic cover of the bottle, the fish can breathe easily.
2. The sentence is correct.
3. Manicurists having emerged only recently in the local market, **clients grow gradually.**
4. **Medical authorities having averted** a medical crisis in the use of antibiotics, the bird flu is the next hurdle.
5. Arabian countries having monopolized the oil market, oil price **tends** to move upwards.
6. Neighbouring countries **having antagonized** one another, trading with one another keeps them together.
7. The sentence is correct.
8. Abductors having beheaded their hostages, terrorists having exploded bombs mindlessly to kill innocent people, both **have** no sense of morality.
9. The sentence is correct.
10. **The critic having drowsed** through the show, a bad review of the film will prevail in **his** column.
11. The rebels, their leader having mustered reinforcements from the countryside, **are advancing** towards the capital to overthrow the government and its army.
12. The sentence is correct.
13. The surgeon, the scalpel having slit open the wound, **tweaked** the bullet from its wedged location.
14. The sentence is correct.
15. The salesman **having plonked** the soda can onto the desk, the spilt liquid wetted a few invoices. [The phrase "**had wetted**" can replace "**wetted**".]

## EXERCISE 6

1. Souvenirs **aplenty** in the glass cabinets, a keen traveller **having traversed** the American continent and European countries, she is now eyeing either Africa or China, a decision still **lingering** in her mind.

2. His reaction **anomalous**, the board **having dismissed** him as the school principal, the veteran educator calmly strode out of the conference room, a few members **approaching** him and **bidding** him farewell.

3. Comrades **waving** hands frantically, the ship **having steered** away from the dock, the old communist leader, eyes **bleary**, shook his right fist in the air.

4. The hot desert **hazardous** to novice explorers, archaeologists **having dug** out historical ruins in the inhospitable land, a romantic adventure awaits the foolhardy or an astute researcher, warm sand **luring** either to death or life in the past.

5. A new fantasy story **invigorating** to the mind, special effects **having mesmerized** television viewers at home in a short preview, the movie spanning two hours, cinemagoers are eagerly booking advance tickets.

6. Resentment of stronger opponents **consuming** her life, the tennis player trains for hours, the coach **supportive** but **wary**, heat exhaustion **having landed** her in hospital once.

7. Heart **throbbing**, her leering **having attracted** the handsome man's attention, she wondered if he would be approaching her, a wish **uncertain** and **elusive**.

8. War correspondents **responsible** and **truthful**, strict censorship **having succumbed** to such noble and brave reporters, a story in the frontline **risking** their life, the camera and pen are their primary weapons.

9. Hands **shivering** a little and icy **cold**, eyes **having shut**, his mind was slipping away.

10. A voice **having summoned** him for dinner, the junior left the playground, sandals **shuffling** towards home, eyes **misty** as he left his friends behind.

# ASSIGNMENT 5

(Submit these exercises for marking and evaluation. Write all your answers on A4 size single-lined papers.)

## EXERCISE 1: PHRASE-WRITING

**Create your own suitable content of the Nominative Absolutes using Active-Continuous Participle Phrase of the given verbs in the locations where these words are placed in the sentences. Remember to include your own subject for each construction.**

Examples:

a.     **brandish** , the clinic doctor complied with the demand to take out the bullet in his abdomen.
 *Answer:* a. *The wounded robber **brandishing** a pistol*, the doctor complied with the demand to take out the bullet in his abdomen.

b.     The convoy with military escort, **straggle** , was moving slowly but cautiously along the dangerous route.
*Answer:* b.  The convoy with military escort, *the refugees **straggling** behind*, was moving slowly but cautiously along the dangerous route.

c.     The boyfriend was coaxing the girl to come down from the parapet, **witness** .
*Answer:* c. The boyfriend was coaxing the girl to come down from the parapet, *many spectators **witnessing** the rooftop drama in horror*.

WRITE OUT THE COMPLETE SENTENCES ON A4 SIZE SINGLE-LINED PAPERS AND UNDERLINE THE NOMINATIVE ABSOLUTES.

1.     **glide** , the guests were marveling at the trendy wedding gowns.
2.     The pickpocket gang, **stride** , panicked
3.     **shuffle** , the grandchildren were occupied with the video games.
4.     The riot police, **shamble** , were protecting the non-strikers against protesters.
5.     Curious villagers are being kept away, **tread** .
6.     The little girl, **coax** , would not close her eyes.
7.     **pore** , the teachers are encouraging them in the canteen.

114

8. **discern** , the door was opened wide for him to enter.
9. **ogle** , the infuriated wife stamped out of the ward.
10. The baby was amused, **peek** .
11. **glare** , the lady was complaining about the taste of the curry fish.
12. **wend** , the low prices were just hard to ignore.
13. Photographers, **strut** , are snapping for the ideal shots.
14. **slouch** , several nurses chatted with him.
15. **embrace** , words of consolation poured out from the relatives.
16. **slink** , tears began to ooze out from his eyes uncontrollably.
17. **babble** , the bartender tried to pacify him.
18. The client's face, **foretell** , was expressing a smile.
19. The furious manager was appeased by the suggestion, **intercede** .
20. **peer** , his nose caught a terrible scent of decay.

## EXERCISE 2: SENTENCE-WRITING

**Write twenty sentences of the Nominative Absolutes using the Active-Continuous Participle Phrases. Include ten Nominative Absolutes using Adjective of your own construction in any of the ten sentences.** Do make use of the vocabulary lists at the end of this manual if you need to.

## EXERCISE 3: PARAGRAPH-WRITING

**Write one Climax of three paragraphs using at least five Nominative Absolutes using Active-Continuous Participle Phrase/Adjective** (you can lengthen the paragraphs to achieve this) and **one paragraph of Conclusion.** Follow the Narrative Essay-Writing guideline as close as possible.

PART 4: **CLIMAX** (3 paragraphs in about 140 words)
　　Describe action situations only to create excitement and anticipation as the character or characters resolved the dilemma.
　　　　(b)　Use Simple Past and Past Continuous Tenses
　　　　(c)　Use Active-Continuous, Active-Perfect, Passive-Continuous, Passive-Perfect and Being Participle Phrases.
　　　　(d)　Use Nominative Absolute constructions with Active-Continuous Participle Phrases/Adjective.

　　Paragraph 1: Long sentences can be used to describe actions (about 60 words).

Paragraph 2: Short sentences should be used to describe fast actions (about 30 words).

Paragraph 3: Long sentences can be used to describe actions (about 50 words).

PART 5:     **CONCLUSION** (1 paragraph about 20 words)
Close the story in any creative way to instill in the reader a lingering thought about the characters.

Example:
*<u>Two courageous firemen **nipping** through the engulfed staircase</u>, the rest gaped apprehensively. <u>The staircase **solid** and **firm**</u>, they were only concerned about the modicum of heat felt through their fireproof suits. The group quickly trudged on towards the moaning, <u>the earnest appeal **having faded** away after a few coughs</u>. <u>A female body **unconscious** and **lying** on the floor in an office amidst the flames</u>, the duo scooted forward.*

*The dense smoke already knocked out the victim a moment before. They grabbed the lady executive. <u>Their eyes **peering** for an open window</u>, one was spotted nearby. They dashed for it.*

***Having failed** to revive her with fresh air, they tied a rope round her waist. <u>Colleagues **waiting** anxiously below, their hands **having grasped** the rope</u>, the firemen let down the unconscious lady gradually. Then they leaped out of the window into the prepared airbags, <u>the floor **collapsing** behind them</u>.*

*They were safe. Loud clapping woke up the rescued lady in the hands of a medical team. She was grateful to the two heroes.*

# EXERCISE 4: ESSAY-WRITING

**Write <u>one</u> narrative essay of 500 words** from the following:

1. How an angry mob was pacified.
2. A city in danger because of an explosion and how it was saved.
3. Saving an animal in danger.
4. Describe how you overcame a phobia.
5. Describe how you helped a person recover from a debt problem.

<u>Alternatively</u>, if you prefer, choose one factual essay below instead:

1. Playing computer games is useful. Do you agree?
2. How should we prepare for a natural disaster?
3. What kind of working life do you prefer?
4. Why do people watch movies?
5. Should a career have more priority over one's family time?

Remember to add Nominative Absolutes using Active-Continuous Participle Phrase/Adjective in your Climax. You can try adding them in your Conversation too but you can practise this later. Active-Continuous and Active-Perfect Participle Phrases are always essential in Suspense and Climax. Adhere to the Narrative essay-writing guideline if a narrative essay topic is chosen. Otherwise, you are free to express the advanced grammar structures in the factual essay wherever you can.

# ASSIGNMENT 6

(Submit these exercises for marking and evaluation. Write all your answers on A4 size single-lined papers.)

## EXERCISE 1: PHRASE-WRITING

**Create your own suitable content of the Nominative Absolutes using Active-Perfect Participle Phrase of the given words in the locations where these words are placed in the sentences. Remember to include your own subject for each construction.**

Examples:

a.  **promenade** , the wide variety of products available impressed them greatly.
*Answer:* a. *The Chinese leaders **having promenaded** in the supermarkets*, the wide variety of products available impressed them greatly.

b.  The anxious daughter, **nuzzle** , received a clear view of the outside through the spot.
*Answer:* b. The anxious daughter, *her nose **having nuzzled** the misty window pane*, received a clear view of the outside through the spot.

c.  The jobseeker is disappointed once again, **scrutinize** .
*Answer:* c. The jobseeker is disappointed once again, *his eyes **having scrutinized** the job advertisements in the newspapers*.

WRITE OUT THE COMPLETE SENTENCES ON A4 SIZE SINGLE-LINED PAPERS AND UNDERLINE THE NOMINATIVE ABSOLUTES.

1.  **yank** , the bolts of the computer casing were quickly removed.
2.  **dandle** , an ice cream seller caught her attention.
3.  The aggressive trespasser, **elbow** , groaned in pain.
4.  **extirpate** , fertilizer was added to enrich the soil with nutrients.
5.  The forensic pathologist discovered a crucial evidence, **scrape** .
6.  The loyal subjects, **embrace** , admired his humility and religious fervour.

7. The famous comedian, **reserve** , rewarded their enthusiasm with great humour.
8. His face turned pale by the gruesome sight, **peep** .
9. The twins are hard to differentiate, **receive** .
10. The distraught miners, **scoot** , were staggering out of the mine in a daze.
11. Job-seekers must display integrity and confidence during the probe, **scan** .
12. The defending lawyer vehemently attempted to discredit the witness, **affect** .
13. **solicit** , a substantial amount is set aside for renting a shop space.
14. **prod** , the dormitory might provide some hiding space.
15. **rive** , its wheels crossed over some debris and flew off the track.
16. The guests, **wring** , observed him put the body in a bag.
17. Some skeptics will scoff at the project, **fail** .
18. The beach lovers, **caress** , may encounter a monstrous tsunami without warning.
19. Monetary compensation is the consequence, **slander** .
20. The sputtering words of a dying testator have little significance, **predetermine.**


# EXERCISE 2: SENTENCE-WRITING

**Write twenty sentences of the Nominative Absolutes using the Active-Perfect Participle Phrases. Include ten Nominative Absolutes using Adjective of your own construction in any sentences.** Do make use of the vocabulary lists at the end of this manual if you need to.


# EXERCISE 3: PARAGRAPH-WRITING

**Write one Climax of three paragraphs using at least five Nominative Absolutes using Active-Perfect Participle Phrase/Active-Continuous Participle Phrase/ Adjective** (you can lengthen the paragraphs to achieve this) **and one paragraph of Conclusion.** Follow the Narrative Essay-Writing guideline as close as possible.

PART 4:   **CLIMAX** (3 paragraphs in about 140 words)
   Describe action situations only to create excitement and anticipation as the character or characters resolved the dilemma.
      (e)   Use Simple Past and Past Continuous Tenses

(f)   Use Active-Continuous, Active-Perfect, Passive-Continuous, Passive-Perfect and Being Participle Phrases.
(g)   Use Nominative Absolute constructions with Active-Continuous and Active-Perfect Participle Phrases.

Paragraph 1: Long sentences can be used to describe actions (about 60 words).
Paragraph 2: Short sentences should be used to describe fast actions (about 30 words).
Paragraph 3: Long sentences can be used to describe actions (about 50 words).

PART 5:   **CONCLUSION** (1 paragraph about 20 words)
Close the story in any creative way to instill in the reader a lingering thought about the characters.

Example:

*The submissive wife **having incurred** the wrath of the raving spouse, vituperative remarks flew at her, **horrifying** the elderly couple. This was not their sweet son anymore – just a reckless drunkard! The man **abusive** and **grasping** a wooden ruler, it broke, **having swiped** the woman's back a few times. **Having vowed** to find another woman who would supply him alcohol, he started to leave the apartment.*

*The careless words enraged the seemingly quiet wife. She kicked his right knee. He fell. The old man **having grabbed** an umbrella, the handle thumped the head twice. The old woman cuffed the cheek.*

*The rambling maniac suddenly came to his senses. The parents **having disclosed** disgust at his impropriety and **threatening** to disown him, he sobbed bitterly. Sobriety **having filtered** into his brain, he apologized profusely to his wife and them. His folly **apparent**, he was a slave to alcoholism.*

*The husband **having reconciled** with his spouse, she would be there with him for his treatment and counselling.*

# EXERCISE 4: ESSAY-WRITING

**Write <u>one</u> narrative essay of 500 words** from the following:

1. Describe a night when you had insomnia.
2. Describe an experience when you were left behind.
3. Write a realistic story of how a losing business became successful.
4. Describe an accident when some people suffered injury in a theme park.
5. Write a realistic story about a comical situation.

<u>Alternatively</u>, if you prefer, choose one factual essay below instead:

1. Which is more important - health or happiness?
2. What are your dreams for a new life if you are dissatisfied with yours now?
3. What are the effects of the increased use of motor vehicles?
4. What is a proper sex education for teenagers these days?
5. What are the things that make you proud of your country?

Remember to add Nominative Absolutes using Active-Continuous Participle Phrase/ Active-Perfect Participle Phrase/Adjective in your Climax. You can try adding them in your Conversation too but you can practise this later. Active-Continuous and Active-Perfect Participle Phrases are always essential in Suspense and Climax. Adhere to the Narrative essay-writing guideline if a narrative essay topic is chosen. Otherwise, you are free to express the advanced grammar structures in the factual essay wherever you can.

# 1.4 WRITING STORIES THAT KEEP READERS IN SUSPENSE

A very effective plan in ensuring that you write a successful story is to follow what most short television series have been doing. Each serial is a complete story and has to retain excitement throughout the show in about one hour. Of course, yours has to be a summary of the essential parts of the story to complete in about 500 words, the usual requirement in an essay writing examination.

Here is an excellent outline of the essential parts including where to put the variety of grammar structures, the paragraphs and the approximate number of words required for each paragraph.

## NARRATIVE ESSAY-WRITING (about 500 words)

PART 1: **SUSPENSE** (3 paragraphs in about 140 words)
Describe action situations only to create excitement and anticipation as the character or characters suffered a dilemma.
    (a) Use Simple Past and Past Continuous Tenses.
    (b) Use Active-Continuous and Active-Perfect Participle Phrases.

Paragraph 1: Long sentences can be used to describe actions (about 60 words).
    (a) Start with a Colon to explain an action or condition of the character.
    (b) Create 3 Verbs + 2 Participle Phrases structure.

Paragraph 2: Short sentences should be used to describe fast actions (about 30 words).

Paragraph 3: Long sentences can be used to describe actions (about 50 words).
    (a) Create 1 Verb + 3 Prepositional Phrases + 2 Participle Phrases structure.

PART 2:   **FLASHBACK** (1 paragraph in about 50 words)
Describe the characters and provide reasons as background information for the suspense.
        (a)    Use Semi-colon to describe contrasting characters by their past actions.
        (b)    Use Past Perfect and Past Perfect Continuous Tenses.
        (c)    Use Noun, Adverb and Adjective Clauses where possible.

PART 3:   **CONVERSATION** (6 paragraphs in about 150 words)
Describe only significant facts that developed an understanding of the issue as revealed by the characters.
        (d)    Use Inverted Commas.
        (e)    Use Nominative Absolutes with Participle Phrases.
        (f)    Use any Present and Future Tenses in the speeches.
        (g)    Use Conditional Clauses in the speeches if possible.
        (h)    Use Simple Past and Past Continuous Tenses in the narration.

Paragraph 1: Introduce the situation involving characters, location and purpose for this conversation. One or two sentences will suffice with some Participle Phrases or Clauses.

Paragraph 2: *"Don't disturb me!" bellowed the irritated pupil, his eyes glaring at the bullies.*

Paragraph 3: *One culprit, their abuse halted by the sudden appearance of the class monitress, retorted, "Here comes your heroine." The timid boy having escaped their grasp at that instant, the three students returned to their seats.*

Paragraph 4: *"If I had not intervened," asserted the spectacled girl, her approach being both sympathetic and firm, "you would have suffered in their hands again. You must learn to stand up for yourself."*

Paragraph 5: *"Unless you were I," responded the timid boy, "you could not understand." Being warned by his father not to get into trouble in the new school, he had to comply as he himself was a bully in a previous school.*

[For paragraphs 2, 3, 4 and 5, actual examples of how to write a variety of inverted commas are given including relevant narration related to each speech.]

Paragraph 6: Show how characters left the scene to end the conversation.

PART 4: **CLIMAX** (3 paragraphs in about 140 words)
Describe action situations only to create excitement and anticipation as the character or characters resolved the dilemma.
- (a) Use Simple Past and Past Continuous Tenses
- (b) Use Active-Continuous and Active-Perfect Participle Phrases.
- (c) Use Nominative Absolutes with Active-Continuous and Active-Perfect Participle Phrases and Adjective.

Paragraph 1: Long sentences can be used to describe actions (about 60 words).
- (a) Include a dash to emphasize a situation.
- (b) Create 3 Verbs + 2 Participle Phrases structure.

Paragraph 2: Short sentences should be used to describe fast actions (about 30 words).

Paragraph 3: Long sentences can be used to describe actions (about 50 words).
- (a) Create 1 Verb + 3 Prepositional Phrases + 2 Participle Phrases structure.

PART 5: **CONCLUSION** (1 paragraph about 20 words)
Close the story in any creative way to instill in the reader a lingering thought about the characters.

[Certain vocabulary lists at the end of this manual are useful in this outline. The verbs from the "Walk" and "Touch" lists are useful in Suspense and Climax. The verbs from the "Say" list are useful in the Conversation.]

## 1.4.1 Suspense & Flashback

PART 1: **SUSPENSE**

Suspense must create a sense of excitement and curiosity as the chaotic or harmful situation arises, leaving out any explanations for the actions as much as possible. Simply visualize the thrilling actions for the reader.

**Example:**

*Jovali **gaped** at the hideous monster: being more than three metres long and almost as thick as a tree trunk he **chopped** down the day before, the menacing creature **was struggling** with its mouth <u>grasping the chicken coop</u>. The chickens, **cackling** away for their dear life in a cacophony of cries, **could** not **escape** out of the cage. **Having wrenched** off a portion of the metal netting, the huge crocodile **jerked** forward, **widened** its gap and **slammed** its teeth on a helpless chicken, **causing** panic among the rest of the feathered preys.*

*The hasty farmer **darted** to the wooden shed to grab hold of the only axe. The weapon being blunt from the day's chopping, his heart **pounded** in anxiety. It **would** merely **bruise** the hard scale. He **would** definitely **be** the next victim after an initial vain assault. The axe in hand, he **must try** to save his food supply. He practically **trudged** back hesitatingly.*

*Being engrossed with its catch, the raider **lay** motionless with its mouth still in the coop **salivating** and **crunching** the juicy meal. Intimidated by the murderous figure, the chickens **were pacing** back and forth, to one corner and then to the next at the rear, being aware that there **was** no escape from death. Jovali, **realizing** his stupidity, cautiously **plodded** forward to slide up the panel at the rear of the cage – it **was** another exit! The usual exit **was** already **torn** away by the monster.*

(a) **Use Simple Past and Past Continuous Tenses.**

In Suspense, focus on each scene at a time as it happened or was happening at that instant. (Note that we can use Present Tenses to describe an imaginative story as if it is happening right now as you write but it can be quite confusing even for an average student. Given a choice, you should use Past

Tenses!) So use only Simple Past and Past Continuous throughout the Suspense. Refer to Paragraph 2 below for examples to see how they can be used effectively in short sentences for fast action.

(b) **Use Active-Continuous and Active-Perfect Participle Phrases.**

Although you have learnt only two active participle phrases, you should realize that there are others besides these two. You probably notice them in the example in Suspense above. Try using them if you feel competent enough. You will learn them soon in the next module.

Paragraph 1: **Long sentences can be used to describe actions.**

(a) **Start with a colon to explain an action or condition of the character.**

The colon is used to explain the state or situation of the subject that is quickly introduced into the story. Both the state and explanation must use a full sentence each. Note that there is no initial capital for the sentence after the colon in this case.

**Examples:**

*The astonished boy peered at the beggar's face: the moonlight being dim, he could not recognize the face of his long lost father who was suffering from amnesia.*

*Firemen were plodding up the staircase in the blazing tower: their masked eyes were blurry and painful, <u>dense smoke and heat **hindering** their vision</u>, and oxygen tank and tools were weighing on their progress.*

*His fiery eyes were glaring at the enemy's movement: revenge being at hand, he must vanquish his opponent once and for all so that there was no chance of another rebellion.*

You must not add any fact after the colon that does not help to explain the situation.

**Example:**

> *The sailors were astounded to see people on an isolated island: their hands **waving** frantically, they were either greeting them or seeking rescue, <u>so the captain of the ship was informed immediately</u>.* (Wrong)

The underlined subordinate clause does not explain the astonishment of the sailors and should be excluded. Write it as a new sentence.

(b)  **Create 3 Verbs + 2 Participle Phrases structure.**

**Example:**

> ***Having collapsed*** *just before the finishing line, the exhausted runner **struggled** to his feet, **hobbled** a few more paces and **won** the marathon, **drawing** loud cheers from the crowd.*

Focus on the three underlined verbs. When three actions are put together in sequence, they help a reader to imagine movement in quick succession. The two participle phrases each on either end add two more actions. So we have five actions in one sentence! Notice the last verb 'won' must have the word 'and' before it. The sentence is usually long but the actions are felt.

**Examples:**

> ***Having arrived*** *late at the delivery station, the muddle-headed dispatch rider **snatched** the address slip from the table, **grabbed** the wrong parcel and **scooted** out to his motor cycle, not **expecting** that his day was going to be ruined even further.*

> ***Having stabbed*** *the hawker with a scraper, the loan shark **gaped** at the falling figure in horror, **dropped** the bloodied weapon and **scurried** out of the food centre, **leaving** behind the wounded man and his monetary collections in a bag.*

> ***Having caught*** *a glimpse of the suspect, the police detective **tailed** the drug smuggler, **called** for reinforcement and **slunk** into a crowd of shoppers, **avoiding** suspicion.*

Paragraph 2: **Short sentences should be used to describe fast actions.**

**Example:**

> The dagger **swung** at his right cheek. He **swerved**. He **felt** a scrape and then a burnt sensation. Red fluid **was oozing** out from the wound. Infuriated, he **lunged** at the assailant. Both **fell** into the drain.

A short paragraph of short sentences can be quite effective in projecting fast actions. You also notice the importance of Simple Past and Past Continuous Tenses here to show immediate action at each scene.

**Example:**

> A sudden creak **came** from the front door. Her hands **froze**. Her heart **was throbbing** faster. She **must hide** from another battering. Her feet **would** not **move**. The drunken spouse **would find** her anyway.

There is not much action here but quick responses or reactions. We can feel the anxiety of the character.

**Example:**

> A bundle of thousand dollar notes **was shoved** into his right hand. His eyes **widened**. He **clasped** the bundle tightly. Memory of the hit-and-run accident **was fading** away. He **saw** only the money.

The paragraph describes how the mind of the character develops within a short time.

Paragraph 3: **Create 1 Verb + 3 Prepositional Phrases + 2 Participle Phrases structure.**

**Example:**

> **Having witnessed** the violent protest, the journalists **wended out of** the unruly mob, **away from** the aggression and **into** a nearby hotel, **intending** to take photographs from a high floor.

Such construction is often complicated because it needs distinct perception to move in the same way through all the three directions. The two Participle Phrases should not be difficult to insert by now.

**Examples:**

***Having peeked** at his grandson, the disgraced politician **slouched** slowly **through** the main gate, **across** the road and **into** a police van, **keeping** his head bowed in humiliation.*

***Having spotted** the immigration officers, the fugitive **bolted across** the busy road, **over** a railing and **into** an alley, **knowing** that he would be expelled from the country after a jail term and some strokes of the cane if he was caught.*

***Having declared** their determination to find the isolated natives, the anthropologists **trod beyond** the known path, **along** a faint trial and further **into** the deep jungle, **slashing** through thick undergrowth and bushes with their parangs (long broad knives).*

PART 2:    **FLASHBACK**

The Flashback actually replaces the introduction of an essay by providing descriptions of the character traits or background details that lead to the Suspense. Do not summarize the whole story here!

Here is an **example** that continues from the Suspense:

*The helpless old man **had been warned** about crocodiles by the villagers who had **been visiting** him once a week to send him supplies. His wife whom he **had squabbled** with frequently **had left** him to stay with their son in the village; the stubborn husband **had refused** to leave the farm which **had been** the source of livelihood all his life. So the farmer **had been** alone for just a week when the anticipated encounter **had begun** though he **had prayed** that his god **would have prevented** it.*

(a)    **Use Semi-colon to describe contrasting characters by their past actions.**

Semi-colon connects main clauses, not subordinate clauses. So they must be capable of becoming complete sentences on their own.

**Example:**

> Recruit Sammy **had been performing** well above the rest as he **had wanted** to be the best trainee in the company; Recruit Pang, a rival, **had slackened** and **would not have been** able to catch up even if he tried; Recruit Lim, although he **had not been** competitive, **had sworn** to be an officer and **would have done** anything to achieve his aim.

(b) **Use Past Perfect and Past Perfect Continuous Tenses.**

Notice the bold words above in the examples above. They are Past Perfect and Past Perfect Continuous Tenses to signify that these events happen before the Suspense. Only a few Perfect Tenses are required in an essay and this is the best place to put them without disrupting the flow of fast actions. However, you must be cautious as Simple Past and Past Continuous Tenses may be needed in certain situations, especially to describe current character traits or events. Avoid this if possible.

**Example:**

> The sea **was** calm and gleaming off light from the sun's ray; its waves **were soothing**, <u>**making** an incessant melodious chain of music</u>. The crew **was** a lethargic lot, <u>**basking** in the sunlight and enjoying the sea breeze</u>. No one **showed** interest in the killer whales; no one thought they **could be menacing** for they **had** often **worked** with men to kill blues whales.

This is not a Flashback but a **Background** description, especially useful in narrative descriptive essay, so a mixture of all Past Tenses is required. You need to be well versed in your tenses to do this. Notice Participle Phrase may be included though you have enough opportunity to do so elsewhere. Only one Adverb Clause exists here which may not be good if no clauses exist elsewhere in the essay.

(c) **Use Noun, Adverb and Adjective Clauses where possible.**

The underlined subordinate clauses above are here to simply tell the reader that you remember them. Participle Phrases may replace many of these clauses but you still need a variety of grammar structures. They are useful here to slow down the pace and start thinking retrospectively, that means looking back at the past events to understand the Suspense situation.

## 1.4.2 Conversation

PART 3: **CONVERSATION**

Conversation is a speech interaction between or among characters. Describe only significant facts in the speeches that develop an understanding of the issue as revealed by the characters. Avoid frivolous or useless conversation.

Here is an **example**:

*A mission which was suicidal from the start, the lone policeman ambled confidently to the armed mob blocking the route out of the province.*

*"Who is the village head here? Who is the leader?"* **inquired** *Sammy, his hands raised in front of them to show that he was not carrying any weapon.*

*A heavily bearded man, <u>his eyes **glaring** at the uniformed figure</u>, **bellowed**, "I am the village head. Who are these people behind you?"*

*"They are innocent villagers,"* **explained** *the calm officer, "whose homes have been destroyed. They are not fighters. They simply want to leave this place just as you wish of them. There's no point harming these frightened people. You can observe that there are old people, women and children with them." <u>His lips **having paused** for a moment</u>, Sammy gazed into the eyes of the old man, whom he prayed would let them through.*

*"Tell them we don't want them back here,"* **warned** *the fiery leader, his voice being heightened to ensure his demand was heard. "They will get hurt if they come back. Then they cannot blame us."*

*The village head being the authoritative figure, the armed mob stepped aside for the convoy of vehicles to pass through. Sammy thanked the wise leader profusely before taking the last vehicle away from the troubled scene.*

Paragraph 1: **Introduce the situation involving characters, location and purpose for this conversation.**

**Example:**

> *Their aim to teach Meng Tuck a lesson for wanting to leave their gang, the five youths cornered him under the staircase in the void deck of his residential block.*

One or two sentences will suffice. The reader does not have to guess who and where the characters are and also why they are having this conversation. We discuss this in the later Module.

(a) **Use Inverted Commas.**

Paragraph 2: **The inverted commas enclose the speech in the front before the "Say" verb.**

**Example:**

> *"Don't hurt me!"* **yelled** *the helpless student, his schoolbag **defending** him against some of the several punches and kicks.*

If the speech is in front, the punctuation at the end of the enclosed sentence can be an exclamation mark, a question mark or a comma but not a full stop. A comma replaces a full stop. There is no more comma after the inverted commas. The underlined sentence is a Nominative Absolute using Active-Continuous Participle Phrase.

Paragraph 3: **The inverted commas enclose the speech at the end behind the "Say" verb.**

**Example:**

> *The gangsters **having savoured** the punishment of the beaten teenager, the leader, Seng Huat, **uttered**, "You can't just leave our gang without paying compensation. Pay us $200 by the end of this week even if you have to steal from your parents or lie to them."*

If the speech is at the end, the punctuation at the end of the enclosed sentence can include a full stop. However, there is a comma after the "Say" verb and before the inverted commas.  Also, notice that there can be more than one sentence in a speech without inserting extra inverted commas.  The underlined sentence is a Nominative Absolute using Active-Perfect Participle Phrase.

Paragraph 4: **The inverted commas enclose both the partial speech in front and the remaining part of the speech at the end, but each set of inverted commas encloses part of a sentence.**

**Example:**

*"I'm not paying you crooks,"* **murmured** *the courageous boy, the voice weakened by the pains felt in his body,* **"a**nd *you all just wait for the police."*

The beginning partial speech ends with a comma.  Notice there is another comma before the inverted commas for the remaining speech.  It is important to note that the beginning word "and" has no initial capital because the remaining speech is a continuation of the beginning speech.  The sentence has been broken into two parts and hence two sets of inverted commas.

Paragraph 5: **The inverted commas enclose both the partial speech in front and the remaining part of the speech at the end, but each set of inverted commas encloses a full sentence.**

**Example:**

*"What did you say?"* **snapped** *Hock Swee, his ears being sharper than the rest. "You dare to call the police. We'll kill you for sure."*

The beginning speech is a full question.  So there is a full stop instead of a comma before the inverted commas for the remaining speech and an initial capital of the beginning word "You".

Paragraph 6: **Show how characters left the scene to end the conversation.**

**Example:**

*Some neighbours being drawn to the scene by the initial cries of the victim, the gang members had to interrupt their intimidation and disperse before their presence.*

Always let the reader know that you have ended the conversation by indicating the reason for it.

### (b) Use Nominative Absolutes with Participle Phrases.

Use Active-Continuous and Active-Perfect Participles Phrases to form the Nominative Absolutes but you can use others if you feel competent enough.

### (c) Use Present and Future Tenses.

Use any suitable tenses in the speeches, especially Present and Future Tenses, since you are using the Past Tenses for most part of the narration. Abbreviated phrases can be used like "I'm", "wouldn't", "can't", "haven't" or "don't". Extra care must be taken in a mixture of many tenses as already observed in all the speeches.

### (d) Use Conditional Clauses in the speeches if possible.

You will practise Conditional Tenses in detail in the next Module. Here you can taste some examples in the speeches and some explanations.

**Example:**

*"If the boss **were** present, he **would tell** me to do the same thing, " blurted the assistant manager, his lips shaking with indignation.*

Since the If-Clause has a Simple Past Tense "were", the subjunctive "would tell" must have a simple infinitive "tell" too. Remember this important rule! However, notice that though the boss is singular, "were" is plural. The word "were" is always used instead of "was" and even "is" or "are" because this is an Unlikely Event Conditional Clause.

**Example:**

*"If you **had been** there," bellowed the irate husband, the wife's complaint having hurt him, "you **would have understood** me"*

Since the If-Clause has a Past Perfect Tense "had been", the subjunctive "would have understood" must have a perfect infinitive "have told" too. Again, remember this important rule! The perfect condition is used to emphasize the situation. Otherwise, simply use a simple condition. Contrast with a similar speech below:

**Example:**

*"If you **were** there," bellowed the irate husband, the wife's complaint having hurt him, "you **would understand** me."*

The speech is mild and probably the simple condition is unsuitable.

(e) **Use Simple Past and Past Continuous Tenses in the narration.**

This is just a reminder that they exist in any Conversation.

## 1.4.3 Climax & Conclusion

PART 4:   **CLIMAX**

Describe action situations only to create excitement and anticipation as the character or characters resolve the dilemma. Avoid confusion here unless you need a Twist in the story. A Twist is an additional dilemma that comes in as a surprise. The Climax is almost the same in structure and strategy as the Suspense, except that more Nominative Absolutes are displayed here:

**Example:**

*<u>The truckloads of exuberant refugees **rolling** calmly along the <u>dusty road</u></u>, the peaceful sight was abruptly shattered by renewed bombardment of army artillery. Panicked old men, women and children, scarce belongings in their grip, scattered out of the stalled vehicles, across the ditches and into the nearby caves on the hillsides for cover**,** **evading** the fatal missiles. All vehicles in the countryside being arbitrarily targeted by the corrupt government forces as belonging to rebel guerillas, the refugees' convoy was not spared.*

*The guns halted almost immediately. Frightened survivors crawled out of the caves. Dead and wounded bodies of several unfortunate refugees on the bloodied ground greeted them. Lamentations and vituperations burst out. The sky painted with billows of smoke, some vehicles were in blazing flames. There was much despair.*

*Twenty army jeeps soon arrived**,** their task to mop up the remaining rebels. Their lives which were once again in danger, the refugees scooted into the caves. Suddenly, hails of bullets rained down from the top of the hillsides. <u>The government soldiers **naïve but relentless**</u>, return fire initiated a massacre. More blood was spilt but the refugees were glad – they were avenged!*

(a)   **Use Simple Past and Past Continuous Tenses.**

(b)   **Use Active-Continuous and Active-Perfect Participle Phrases.**

Refer to earlier explanations.

(c)  **Use Nominative Absolute constructions with Participle Phrases.**

Use the Active-Continuous and Active-Perfect Participle Phrases for the Nominative Absolutes unless you simply want to try the others – just from observing the given examples.

Paragraph 1: **Long sentences can be used to describe actions.**

(a)  **Include a dash to emphasize a situation.**

**Examples:**

*The waiters skate their way to the customers' tables* **- balancing dishes and wending through tables and customers.**

*The nervous drug courier was fidgeting with the luggage to ensure they were locked* – **a suspicious action that alerted a custom officer.**

The emphatic statement for the dash needs not be a full sentence. Just remember to put the dash a little further from the words so that it does not look like a hyphen. The dash with its emphatic words is an insertion in a proper sentence.

**Examples:**

*The baby* – **its tantrum getting worse** – *was bawling out for attention in the middle of the night.*

*The refugees* – **smoke billowing from burning vehicles and buildings behind them** - *were plodding along the dusty road towards shelter.*

Double dashes can be used to enclose the emphatic statement.

(b) **Create 3 Verbs + 2 Participle Phrases structure.**

**Examples:**

*A pair of scissors **having struck** her head*, the flustered lady **staggered** a few paces, **sensed** pain and giddiness, and **sat** on the floor in the void deck, *the hair **wet** with blood **oozing** out of the wound.*

*A salesman **aggressive** and **stalking** a shopper*, a security guard in the mall **halted** his pursuit, **questioned** his business conduct and **demanded** his identification, *a failure to comply **resulting** in his expulsion from the premises.*

Nominative Absolutes replace participle phrases.

Paragraph 2: **Short sentences should be used to describe fast actions.**

**Examples:**

*A flashlight beamed into the basement. Small bodies seemed to slide away. Then the light captured a few. Figures **embracing** each other, their faces displayed fear. They were the missing children!*

*The safe was open. The money was gone. The partner **having betrayed** him, the entrepreneur was furious. A police report was made. Attempts to find the partner and money were in vain. Then he realized he needed to trust his brother.*

Nominative Absolute can be added in a paragraph of short sentences.

Paragraph 3: **Create 1 Verb + 3 Prepositional Phrases + 2 Participle Phrases structure.**

**Examples:**

*A bull terrier **on** his scent, the trespasser **scrambled to** the locked main gate, **over** it and **away from** the scene, the barking **having aroused** the owner's attention.*

*His body **in** camouflage, the sniper **slithered under** the fence, **along** a muddy patch and **into** a bush, his mind **focusing** on the target rather than his own safety.*

Nominative Absolutes replace participle phrases.

PART 5:     **CONCLUSION**

Close the story in any creative way to instill in the reader a lingering thought about the characters. The following is a continuation from the Climax.

**Example:**

*Rebel guerillas vanished as quickly as they appeared. The refugees exhausted and **reeling** from their physical and mental wounds, volunteer workers took time to help them bury their dead and bandage their wounds before urging them on. The damaged but functional vehicles and stragglers finally plodded along the road to safety – a refugee camp protected by United Nations forces located across the border.*

The dilemma already resolved, conclude by looking at the consequence of the Climax.

**Examples:**

*The dead crocodile **towering** above the height of the fragile old farmer as it was hanging from a tree branch, crowds of spectators from the village arrived to admire the aged hero's feat in protecting his chickens including his concerned wife, son and grandchildren. They were secretly proud of him though his wife kept reminding him that he was a foolish old man.*

*The handcuffed extortionists being led away by undercover detectives to a police van, the police sergeant patted the courageous boy on the shoulder while the father was grasping the cold sweaty hand of his son. Words were not spoken but the son knew that his father had been anxious for his safety.*

@@@@@@@@@@@@@@@@@@@@@@@@@@@@@@@@

Refer to Self-Practice 1.4 and Assignments 7 & 8 to complete the exercises there.

@@@@@@@@@@@@@@@@@@@@@@@@@@@@@@@@

# SELF-PRACTICE 1.4

(These Exercises Should Be Done Before The Assignments. Do Not Submit Them As Answers Are Provided At The End.)

EXERCISE 1: WHAT ARE MISSING?   SHARPENING YOUR SENTENCES!

**Fill in the missing punctuations (capital letter, full-stop, exclamation mark, question mark, colon, dash or enclosed dashes, comma or enclosed commas and enclosed inverted commas)** and **construct a Participle Phrase or Nominative Absolute by transforming the <u>underlined words</u>** and put it in the same location where you find it.

Examples:

a.   There is no truth in that statement asserted the defendant <u>his eyes were glaring at the witness</u>.
*Answer:* a.   *"There is no truth in that statement!" asserted the defendant, <u>his eyes **glaring** at the witness</u>.*

b.   Onlookers gaped at the bloody body <u>blood was oozing out from its slit neck</u> the body was still shaking continuously he was already dead.
*Answer:* b.   Onlookers gaped at the bloody body: <u>blood oozing out from its slit neck</u>, the body was still shaking continuously – he was already dead.

WRITE OUT YOUR ANSWERS ON ANY A4 SIZE SINGLE-LINED PAPERS.

1.   Fishermen were astonished at the unusual sight <u>the water was receding much further away from the beach</u> fishes, seaweeds, and a lot of junk were stranded on the bed.

2.   The tiger was stalking a deer in the open field <u>its eyes were focusing on the prey</u> the predator ambled confidently forward.

3.   The hornets appear menacing they are swarming all over their hive in a massive force <u>they are securing the safety of their home against a pest control team</u>.

4. Young fearless warriors the leopards of the tribe would face the enemy fighters in armed combat to determine victory or defeat <u>they face the challenge with pride.</u>

5. <u>After the investor had carped on his stock losses he</u> swore he would not speculate on shares anymore a promise he was never able to keep.

6. <u>Ancient prophecies are predicting the end of the world they</u> face modern skeptics the technologists of a futuristic world.

7. Fireflies glow in the dark blurted a two year old boy <u>who was grinning widely</u> they run on batteries

8. The sick patient <u>his bluish lips were quivering</u> sputtered help I…can't…breathe

9. We've pledged to watch out for each other uttered the superintendent sadly <u>he was slouching towards the conference room</u> even though we are on different sides of the law.

10. <u>The class monitor had accused the new student of theft he</u> accentuated he's the last person to leave the class for recess

11. If a computer engineer were here alleged the brother <u>who had maliciously erased the sister's hard disk</u> he could not save your data too.

12. If your peers had corrupted your morals retorted the counsellor <u>a frown was emerging from the forehead</u> you would have been responsible too.

13. <u>Her rebuttal had silenced the complainant</u> the arbitrator resolved it seems to me that the complaint is not valid and the case should be dismissed.

14. Fortify yourself for the worst lamented the uncle <u>his sharp eyes had noticed a reddish glow in the dark sky at a distance</u> the factory is probably gone.

15. Why are you here in the shop probed the security guard <u>while he was discerning that something was amiss</u> I don't see your boss around.

16. Aren't we all slaves to work contended the debater <u>his wittiness was amusing the audience</u> whether we work for money or survival we cannot evade work

17. Don't jeopardize your future censured the factory spokesman <u>after he had mollified the strikers at the gate</u> return to work and we can negotiate again in a reasonable manner.

18. There must be give and take interceded the mediator <u>his proposal was stirring up some uneasiness</u> or else both of you may lose more money in a legal suit.

19. We are still poor incited the activist <u>his voice was blasting at the crowd through a loudhailer</u> because the government is corrupt.

20. I'm a terrorist prattled a tourist <u>a few spies were listening close by</u> because I don't like American troops in Iraq.


EXERCISE 2: GETTING MORE ACTIONS IN ONE SENTENCE!

**Combine the sentences into one sentence** with either of the following structures:
(a)   **3 Verbs + 2 Participle Phrases**, or
(b)   **1 Verb + 3 Prepositional Phrases + 2 Participle Phrases**



Examples:

a.   The lady wore high heels for the first time. She stumbled out of the shop. She staggered a few paces along the pavement. She reeled forward. She felt flustered.
*Answer:* a. **Having worn** *high heels for the first time, the lady* <u>stumbled</u> *out of the shop,* <u>staggered</u> *a few paces along the pavement and* <u>reeled</u> *forward,* **feeling** *flustered.*

b.   The desperate wife ensured that she was not shadowed. She strode rapidly through a crowd of shoppers. She walked quickly into an alley. She came out to another busy street. She was glancing back once a while.
*Answer:* b. **Having ensured** *that she was not shadowed, the desperate wife* <u>strode</u> *rapidly* <u>through</u> *a crowd of shoppers,* <u>into</u> *an alley and* <u>out to</u> *another busy street,* **glancing** *back once a while.*

1.     The policewoman coaxed the suicidal teenager to come nearer to the window.  Then she stepped onto the ledge.  She slithered towards the sobbing figure.  She projected her hand while she was anticipating the confused girl would grasp her hand in response.

2.     The mother swiped the daughter's leg once.  She squinted at the teenager through her eyeglasses.  She perceived the tears welling up in her eyes.  She dropped the new rattan cane.  She regretted her hasty act.

3.     The bicyclist was determined to catch up with his friends at the junction.  He raced down the sloping pathway.  He wended through a few shocked pedestrians.  He collided with his friend's stationary bicycle.  He was ignoring all safety rules.

4.     The undergraduates alighted from the bus.  They scurried out of the bus-stop shelter.  They ran across puddles of water on the wet pavement.  They hurried to the school building.  They drenched themselves in the heavy downpour.

5.     The zoologists hauled the crocodile out of the truck.  They plodded through the thick undergrowth.  They lumbered down the riverbank and into the swamp.  They intended to release the creature into its own domain.

6.     The pickpocket clinched a wallet.  He slunk away from the victim.  He walked through a crowd. He sneaked into a restaurant.  He attempted to check its content immediately.

7.     The motorist spontaneously decided to avert a collision with a stationary van.  He swerved to the right.  He went over the middle line.  He drove into an oncoming traffic.  He was putting himself in greater danger.

8.     The tactical police team pounded down the front door of the three-storey townhouse.  They scooted through the living room.  They dashed up the stairs to the top floor.  They darted into the bedroom.  However, they dreaded the possibility of a dead hostage.

9.     The young explorer bravely crept the cave without torchlight.  He stumbled along in the dark.  He staggered across some rocks.  He reeled clumsily to the ground.  He messed up his clothes and backpack.

10.	The dog sniffed drugs in the vehicle.  It leaped up and down the back seat.  It pulled at the lease.  It dragged the handler to the boot of the car.  It was barking relentlessly.


EXERCISE 3: WHAT'S WRONG?

**Correct all the errors** in the sentences.  You do not need to write out the sentences.

1.	A volunteer having adopted an orphan from the disaster area, a reporter queried "is it ethical?"
2.	The marine police cruised near the beach for the man-eater: the great white shark.
3.	"Let's say you are my husband," hinted the lady colleague, "can we still be friends?"
4.	Having headed the ball into the goal, the soccer player leaped over a player's back, dashed towards the spectators, danced in the field, yelling exuberantly.
5.	"If the transport had failed to bring relief supplies," revealed the army general.  "Many more people would have died in the mountains."
6.	The lecturer was droning on a section of the company law, an undergraduate drawled, "Is he going to end soon?"
7.	Having crashed the stolen car, the thief darted across the road and over a railing, into an alley, evading the eyes of witnesses.
8.	"Sex before marriage is premature," expounded the speaker. "Especially for teenagers and even youths."
9.	"National service is a patriotic act," insisted a forum writer, "therefore, evading it is a sign of disloyalty to the nation."
10.	The citizens are shocked: their king has decided to abdicate three years later and so they are protesting against his decision.
11.	The sisters – Mary and Adeline – are caring youths who do charitable work every Saturday afternoon.
12.	The forest fires are razing precious undiscovered plants – particularly plants that can be used for medicinal herbs and drugs.
13.	Having knocked his foot against the kerb, the pedestrian stumbled onto the pavement, limped a few paces and seated himself at the outdoor section of a café, cursing his bad luck.
14.	Having alerted the police with a careless telephone call to his wife, the escaped convict slunk away from the telephone booth near his home, through a

crowd of bargain hunters at a makeshift stall and into a waiting taxi, aiming to avoid arrest at all cost.

15. Having summoned the mob of soccer hooligans, the activist incited them to burnt vehicles, broke window panes of shops and fought with the police, celebrating their victory win in a soccer match.

@@@@@@@@@@@@@@@@@@@@@@@@@@@@@@

Check your answers at the end. Refer to Assignment 7 and complete the exercises there for submission before you continue with the next exercises here.

@@@@@@@@@@@@@@@@@@@@@@@@@@@@@@

## EXERCISE 4: NARRATIVE ESSAY

**Fill in the missing punctuations (capital letter, full-stop, exclamation mark, question mark, colon, dash or enclosed dashes, comma or enclosed commas and enclosed inverted commas), missing verbs in the blanks** and **construct a Participle Phrase or Nominative Absolute for the underlined words.** **You are free to place any grammar structure in any location according to the text.**

WRITE OUT THE WHOLE CORRECTED ESSAY ON A4 SIZE SINGLE-LINED PAPER.

### KITE FIGHTING AND CHASING KITES

The children were pursuing a kite <u>as the floating prize was towing a loose string</u> they were determined to be that lucky catcher. <u>They focused their eyes on the gliding object</u>. They nipped across busy traffic. They leaped over open drains. They scooted into back alleys. <u>They were forsaking safety</u>. I was one of those neighbourhood kids <u>who enjoyed kite fighting and chased after fallen kites</u>.

The string was lingering in the air in a back alley. A fortunate boy noticed it. <u>His movement towards it was calm and gradual</u>. <u>He eyed it till it was within his reach</u>. He clinched it quickly.

However, the elder brother ruthlessly stole it. <u>He bawled out in vain</u>. The sobbing boy stalked furiously out of the alley. He crossed a road. He walked towards a terrace house. <u>He threatened to report the misdeed</u>. Soon a lanky man <u>who was clutching a lengthy thick cane</u> was yelling for the elder son. <u>It was an amusing sight rather than a violent one</u>.

While enthusiastic fliers _____(criss-cross) their kites in the sky, a glass-laced string _____(cut) the loser's lease. That _____(free) the kite to find another master whose destiny _____(lead) him to it. Remarkably, the children _____ often _____(obey) such unwritten rule. That the elder brother _____(commit) treachery had not surprised me too.

<u>As I had evaded the tussle between father and son</u>, I sought out a Malay kite maker <u>who was residing in a zinc hut behind my terrace dwelling</u>.

cross two light thin rattan strips on the diamond shaped paper instructed the skinny man, as his two hands were bending the horizontal strip and wrap the paper round this one at the ends to hold it

what glue do you use I enquired keenly, because I had noticed the sticky white stuff on the paper where the sticks were placed.

the maker as he was chuckling briefly responded cooked white rice with water will stick when the paste dries up it's cheaper

how about the string blurted another young purchaser I want my kite to be invincible

the glass from the fluorescent lamp is finer revealed the man while his eyebrows were frowning in deep thought.

I released a coin in the expert's hand. I strode back home the proud owner of four new kites.

My mother's starch and finely pounded glass from a fluorescent lamp had created a potent brew. I stirred a roll of thick thread in the heated mixture. I hung out the glass-laced string to dry. I finally rolled my new weapon round a tin. I was imaging a great victory. I trudged to the open space at the back of my house. A few boys were lingering there and were reluctant to go home.

The elder brother, while his kite was dominating the sky, was present. He prated about the few victories earlier. My kite rose rapidly. It had captured a strong current. It darted here and there. It cut a string. The bully's kite flew away. A frown was discernible on his forehead.

His pride yielded to my first victory. The arrogant boy slouched to me. He flattered me on my triumph. He gazed at the thick string. He was imploring me to let him try. Apprehensively, I surrendered to his pleading. I regretted it. All my kites had flown off after a few battles. It was back to chasing kites.

The pastime of chasing kites ended that day with a few stitches on my foot that had stepped on a broken porcelain piece during a chase. A scar on the sole still exists today although a reminiscence is painful but unforgettable.

EXERCISE 5:  LETTER WRITING

**Construct Participle Phrases and Nominative Absolutes using the <u>underlined words</u> and fill in the parentheses (__) with the necessary punctuations.**

WRITE OUT THE WHOLE CORRECTED LETTER ON A4 SIZE SINGLE-LINED PAPER.

December 25, 2005

The Editor
Straits Times Forum

<u>DEATH PENALTY – A NECESSARY EVIL IN AN EVIL WORLD?</u>

We, <u>as we deplore the taking of an innocent life</u>, need not be apologetic in having the death penalty as if we are less mature in morality and spirituality. <u>A secular government has pragmatically perceived a life for a life being fair and just.</u> <u>It has viewed the death penalty as an effective deterrence against murderers, gun-toting robbers and drug traffickers</u>. It has no logical reason to alter course especially in a predominantly Asian society. Though a multi-religious society too, <u>in which the majority of Singaporeans practise Buddhism</u>, the major religions here have no qualms with the death penalty to ensure a safe, healthy and friendly social environment.

<u>As we observe closely</u>, we can see that the cry for the abolition of the death penalty usually comes from Western countries with a large Christian population. <u>God-fearing and people-loving Christians are willing to see one sinner repent so that heaven can rejoice</u>. The life of a criminal is worth saving no matter how evil the crime may be. <u>These Christians discern the death of Jesus Christ on the cross as a sign of God's love</u>. Yet they fail to see the evil of sin, <u>of which the cross is representing too</u>, that took the life of their Saviour. Without the death penalty <u>that reflects the evil of taking away an innocent life</u>, people will be blinded from knowing what great evil has been done!

Rehabilitation does not necessarily result in the removal of retribution (__) a life for a life. <u>While the death sentence is hanging over his head</u>, the criminal usually has time for repentance and restoration of his soul to God's keeping. <u>After he has truly rehabilitated</u>, he is prepared to meet his Maker honestly and courageously. Conversely, <u>since he is serving merely life imprisonment</u>, he may appear well behaved so as to be in good relations with his captors or to get a pardon from the President. Circumstances may possibly arise in the right political climate.

The death penalty is not simply about retribution or restitution although the victim's family most probably recognizes it as such. What if the victim has forgiven the murderer in his dying breath or the victim's family is willing to accept blood money as compensation (__) should not the prisoner be released too (__) Others think society is exacting retribution or demanding restitution since the victim was also a member of the community and, therefore, the punishment is fair and equitable.

The death penalty should not simply be about deterrence especially in the minds of non-criminals (__) only criminals should fear the death sentence. As ordinary citizens have condoned the capital punishment through their support of the government, taking away a life must be seen to be morally and spiritually correct, not just politically. Singaporeans should not feel guilty or ashamed after each hanging. Some foreign media and Western politicians are making wild accusations at Singapore in that it belittles the value of human life and acts as a savage.

The death penalty is not simply about social policy. What if society believes in the reformation of the criminal or that the criminal is evil because of his evil social environment (__) The government protects society with the death penalty. Do we then need a referendum to determine whether society wants protection or the evidence of sociologists to determine if the accused is badly influenced by society (__) Since an evil society has produced an evil criminal, is not this a mitigating factor against the death sentence (__)

The death penalty does represent a high moral principle (__) that every individual's life is worthy especially the innocent victim's (__) so that no one can take it away, or else the offender must forfeit his own life. He has unjustly taken another's life away. The death penalty emphasizes the sanctity of life in an evil world. Activists against the death penalty are blindly focusing on he criminal's life and fail to value the life of the innocent victim. They belittle the latter's life instead.

Human rights activists think they are on high moral ground since no universal social contract has existed for the death penalty. Even though there is no international law for the death penalty, there is also none against it (__) the sovereign states have to decide what works for them. Myriad societies on this

<u>planet hold widely different convictions</u>. An international convention for or against the death penalty cannot exist.

<u>Individual human rights activists claim it is a universal human right principle that life must be preserved at all costs</u>. Before a criminal can claim that his life is precious, he must first preserve the life of his intended victim.

[Your Name]


@@@@@@@@@@@@@@@@@@@@@@@@@@@@@@

Check your answers at the end. If you are ready, refer to Assignment 8 and complete the exercises there for final submission.

@@@@@@@@@@@@@@@@@@@@@@@@@@@@@@

# Answers for Self-Practice 1.4

## EXERCISE 1

1. Fishermen were astonished at the unusual sight: <u>the water **receding** much further away from the beach</u>, fishes, seaweeds, and a lot of junk were stranded on the bed.

2. The tiger was stalking a deer in the open field: <u>its eyes **focusing** on the prey</u>, the predator ambled confidently forward.

3. The hornets appear menacing: they are swarming all over their hive in a massive force, <u>**securing** the safety of their home against a pest control team</u>.

4. Young fearless warriors – the leopards of the tribe – would face the enemy fighters in armed combat to determine victory or defeat, <u>**facing** the challenge with pride</u>.

5. <u>**Having carped** on his stock losses</u>, the investor swore he would not speculate on shares anymore – a promise he was never able to keep.

6. Ancient prophecies, <u>**predicting** the end of the world</u>, face modern skeptics – the technologists of a futuristic world.

7. "Fireflies glow in the dark," blurted a two year old boy, <u>**grinning** widely</u>. "They run on batteries!"

8. The sick patient, <u>his bluish lips **quivering**</u>, sputtered, "Help! I…can't…breathe!"

9. "We've pledged to watch out for each other," uttered the superintendent sadly, <u>**slouching** towards the conference room</u>, "even though we are on different sides of the law."

10. <u>**Having accused** the new student of theft</u>, the class monitor accentuated, "He's the last person to leave the class for recess!"

11. "If a computer engineer were here," alleged the brother, <u>**having** maliciously **erased** the sister's hard disk</u>, "he could not save your data too."

12. "If your peers had corrupted your morals," retorted the counsellor, <u>a frown **emerging** from the forehead</u>, "you would have been responsible too."

13. <u>Her rebuttal **having silenced** the complainant</u>, the arbitrator resolved, "It seems to me that the complaint is not valid and the case should be dismissed."

14. "Fortify yourselves for the worst!" lamented the uncle, <u>his sharp eyes **having noticed** a reddish glow in the dark sky at a distance</u>. "The factory is probably gone."

15. "Why are you here in the shop?" probed the security guard, <u>**discerning** that something was amiss</u>. "I don't see your boss around."

16. "Aren't we all slaves to work?" contended the debater, <u>his wittiness **amusing** the audience</u>. "Whether we work for money or survival, we cannot evade work!"

17. "Don't jeopardize your future!" censured the factory spokesman, <u>**having mollified** the strikers at the gate</u>. "Return to work and we can negotiate again in a reasonable manner."

18. "There must be give and take," interceded the mediator, <u>his proposal **stirring** up some uneasiness</u>, "or else both of you may lose more money in a legal suit."

19. "We are still poor," incited the activist, <u>his voice **blasting** at the crowd through a loudhailer</u>, "because the government is corrupted."

20. "I'm a terrorist," prattled a tourist, <u>a few spies **listening** close by</u>, "because I don't like American troops in Iraq."

## EXERCISE 2

1. **Having coaxed** the suicidal teenager to come nearer to the window, the policewoman <u>stepped</u> onto the ledge, <u>slithered</u> towards the sobbing figure and <u>projected</u> her hand, **anticipating** the confused girl would grasp her hand in response.

2.	**Having swiped** the daughter's leg once, the mother <u>squinted</u> at the teenager through her eye-glasses, <u>perceived</u> the tears welling up in her eyes and <u>dropped</u> the new rattan cane, **regretting** her hasty act.

3.	**Having determined** to catch up with his friends at the junction, the bicyclist <u>raced</u> down the sloping pathway, <u>wended</u> through a few shocked pedestrians and <u>collided</u> with his friend's stationary bicycle, **ignoring** all safety rules.

4.	**Having alighted** from the bus, the undergraduates <u>scurried</u> <u>out of</u> the bus-stop shelter, <u>across</u> puddles of water on the wet pavement and <u>to</u> the school building, **drenching** themselves in the heavy downpour.

5.	**Having hauled** the crocodile out of the truck, the zoologists <u>plodded</u> <u>through</u> the thick undergrowth, <u>down</u> the riverbank and <u>into</u> the swamp, **intending** to release the creature into its own domain.

6.	**Having clinched** a wallet, the pickpocket <u>slunk</u> <u>away from</u> the victim, <u>through</u> a crowd and <u>into</u> a restaurant, **attempting** to check its content immediately.

7.	**Having** spontaneously **decided** to avert a collision with a stationary van, the motorist <u>swerved</u> <u>to</u> the right, <u>over</u> the middle line and <u>into</u> an oncoming traffic, **putting** himself in greater danger.

8.	**Having pounded** down the front door of the three-storey townhouse, the tactical police team <u>scooted</u> <u>through</u> the living room, <u>up</u> the stairs to the top floor and <u>into</u> the bedroom, **dreading** the possibility of a dead hostage.

9.	**Having** bravely **crept** into the cave without torchlight, the young explorer <u>stumbled</u> along in the dark, <u>staggered</u> across some rocks and <u>reeled</u> clumsily to the ground, **messing** up his clothes and backpack.

10.	**Having sniffed** drugs in the vehicle, the dog <u>leaped</u> up and down the back seat, <u>pulled</u> at the lease and <u>dragged</u> the handler to the boot of the car, **barking** relentlessly.

EXERCISE 3

1. A volunteer having adopted an orphan from the disaster area, a reporter **queried,** "is it ethical?"
2. The marine police cruised near the beach for the man-eater **- the great white shark.**
3. "Let's say you are my husband," hinted the lady **colleague.** "can we still be friends?"
4. Having headed the ball into the goal, the soccer player leaped over a player's back, dashed towards the **spectators and danced** in the field, yelling exuberantly.
5. "If the transport had failed to bring relief supplies," revealed the army **general, "many** more people would have died in the mountains."
6. The lecturer **droning** on a section of the company law, an undergraduate drawled, "Is he going to end soon?"
7. Having crashed the stolen car, the thief darted **across the road, over a railing and into an alley**, evading the eyes of witnesses.
8. "Sex before marriage is premature," expounded the **speaker, "especially** for teenagers and even youths."
9. "National service is a patriotic act," insisted a forum writer, "**and, therefore**, evading it is a sign of disloyalty to the nation."
10. The citizens are shocked: their king has decided to abdicate three years **later.**
11. The sisters**, Mary and Adeline,** are caring youths who do charitable work every Saturday afternoon.
12. The sentence is correct.
13. The sentence is correct.
14. The sentence is correct.
15. Having summoned the mob of soccer hooligans, the activist incited them to **burn** vehicles, **break** window panes of shops and **fight** with the police, celebrating their victory win in a soccer match.

EXERCISE 4

The following answer seemingly appearing adequate with just two types of Participle Phrase and three types of Nominative Absolute, a better essay can be written with more variety:

   The children were pursuing a kite: <u>the floating prize **towing** a loose string</u>, they were determined to be that lucky catcher.  **Having focused** their eyes on the gliding object, they <u>nipped</u> across busy traffic, <u>leaped</u> over open drains and <u>scooted</u> into back alleys, <u>forsaking</u> safety.  I was one of those neighbourhood kids **enjoying** kite fighting and **chasing** after fallen kites.

   The string was lingering in the air in a back alley.  A fortunate boy noticed it, <u>his movement towards it **calm** and **gradual**</u>.  **Eyeing** it till it was within his reach, he clinched it quickly.

   However, the elder brother ruthlessly stole it.  **Having bawled** out in vain, the sobbing boy <u>stalked</u> furiously <u>out of</u> the alley, <u>across</u> a road and <u>towards</u> a terrace house, **threatening** to report the misdeed.  Soon a lanky man **clutching** a lengthy thick cane was yelling for the elder son, <u>a sight **amusing** rather than **violent**</u>.

   While enthusiastic fliers <u>had been criss-crossing</u> their kites in the sky, a glass-laced string <u>had cut</u> the loser's lease.  That <u>had freed</u> the kite to find another master whose destiny <u>had led</u> him to it.  Remarkably, the children <u>had</u> often <u>obeyed</u> such unwritten rule.  That the elder brother <u>had committed</u> treachery <u>had not surprised</u> me too.

   **Having evaded** the tussle between father and son, I sought out a Malay kite maker **residing** in a zinc hut behind my terrace dwelling.

   "Cross two light thin rattan strips on the diamond shaped paper, " instructed the skinny man, <u>his two hands **bending** the horizontal strip</u>, "and wrap the paper round this one at the ends to hold it."

   "What glue do you use?" I enquired keenly, **having noticed** the sticky white stuff on the paper where the sticks were placed.

   The maker, **chuckling** briefly, responded, "Cooked white rice with water will stick when the paste dries up.  It's cheaper!"

"How about the string?" blurted another young purchaser. "I want my kite to be invincible!"

"The glass from the fluorescent lamp is finer, " revealed the man, his eyebrows **frowning** in deep thought.

**Having released** a coin in the expert's hand, I strode back home – the proud owner of four new kites.

My mother's starch and finely pounded glass from a fluorescent lamp **having created** a potent brew, I stirred a roll of thick thread in the heated mixture, hung out the glass-laced string to dry and finally rolled my new weapon round a tin, **imagining** a great victory. I trudged to the open space at the back of my house, a few boys l**ingering** there and **reluctant** to go home.

The bullying elder brother, his kite **dominating** the sky, was present. He prated about the few victories earlier. My kite rose rapidly, **having captured** a strong current. It darted here and there. It cut a string. The bully's kite flew away, a frown **discernible** on his forehead.

His pride **having yielded** to my first victory, the loser slouched to me, flattered me on my triumph, and gazed at the thick string, **imploring** me to let him try. Apprehensively, I surrendered to his pleading. I regretted it. All my kites **having flown** off after a few battles, it was back to chasing kites.

The pastime of chasing kites ended that day with a few stitches on my foot **having stepped** on a broken porcelain piece. A scar on the sole, a reminiscence **painful** but **unforgettable**, still exists today.

EXERCISE 5

The following answer scoring more on content points and also language points with the use of two types of Participle Phrase and three types of Nominative Absolute, facts must be studied and remembered for a factual essay.

December 25, 2005

The Editor
Straits Times Forum

DEATH PENALTY – A NECESSARY EVIL IN AN EVIL WORLD?

We, **deploring** the taking of an innocent life, need not be apologetic in having the death penalty as if we are less mature in morality and spirituality. A secular government pragmatically **having perceived** a life for a life being fair and just and **having viewed** the death penalty as an effective deterrence against murderers, gun-toting robbers and drug traffickers, it has no logical reason to alter course especially in a predominantly Asian society. Though a multi-religious society too, the majority of Singaporeans **practising** Buddhism, the major religions here have no qualms with the death penalty to ensure a safe, healthy and friendly social environment.

**Observing** closely, we can see that the cry for the abolition of the death penalty usually comes from Western countries with a large Christian population. God-fearing and people-loving Christians **willing** to see one sinner repent so that heaven can rejoice, the life of a criminal is worth saving no matter how evil the crime may be. These Christians **discerning** the death of Jesus Christ on the cross as a sign of God's love, they fail to see the evil of sin, the cross **representing** it too, that took the life of their Saviour. Without the death penalty **reflecting** the evil of taking away an innocent life, people will be blinded from knowing what great evil has been done!

Rehabilitation does not necessarily result in the removal of retribution – a life for a life. The death sentence **hanging** over his head, the criminal usually has time for repentance and restoration of his soul to God's keeping. **Having** truly **rehabilitated**, he is prepared to meet his Maker honestly and courageously. Conversely, **serving** merely life imprisonment, he may appear well behaved so as to be in good relations with his captors or to get a pardon from the President, circumstances possibly **arising** in the right political climate.

The death penalty is not simply about retribution or restitution, the victim's family most probably **recognizing** it as such.  What if the victim has forgiven the murderer in his dying breath or the victim's family is willing to accept blood money as compensation - should not the prisoner be released too?  Others think society is exacting retribution or demanding restitution, the punishment **fair and equitable** as the victim was also a member of the community.

The death penalty should not simply be about deterrence especially in the minds of non-criminals; only criminals should fear the death sentence.  Ordinary citizens **having condoned** the capital punishment through their support of the government, taking away a life must be seen to be morally and spiritually correct, not just politically.  Singaporeans should not feel guilty or ashamed after each hanging, some foreign media and Western politicians **making** wild accusations at Singapore **belittling** the value of human life and **acting** as a savage.

The death penalty is not simply about social policy.  What if society believes in the reformation of the criminal or that the criminal is evil because of his evil social environment?  The government protecting **society** with the death penalty, do we then need a referendum to determine whether society wants protection or the evidence of sociologists to determine if the accused is badly influenced by society? An evil society **having produced** an evil criminal, is not this a mitigating factor against the death sentence?

The death penalty does represent a high moral principle - that every individual's life is worthy especially the innocent victim's - so that no one can take it away, or else the offender must forfeit his own life, **having** unjustly **taken** another's life away.  The death penalty emphasizes the sanctity of life in an evil world.  Activists against the death penalty, blindly f**ocusing** on he criminal's life, fail to value the life of the innocent victim, **belittling** the latter's life instead.

Human rights activists think they are on high moral ground, no universal social contract **having existed** for the death penalty.  Even though there is no international law for the death penalty, there is also none against it – the sovereign states have to decide what works for them.  Myriad societies on this planet **holding** widely different convictions, an international convention for or against the death penalty cannot exist.

Individual human rights activists **claiming** it is a universal human right principle that life must be preserved at all costs, before a criminal can claim that his life is precious, he must first preserve the life of his intended victim.

[Your Name]

# ASSIGNMENT 7

(Submit these exercises for marking and evaluation. Write all your answers on A4 size single-lined papers.)

## EXERCISE 1: SENTENCE-WRITING (1)

**Construct five sentences using a colon and five sentences using a dash or enclosed dashes.** Create your own content. The underlined Nominative Absolute is optional.

Examples:

a. The family members stuck to their chairs**:** things *falling* to the floor which was vibrating along with the walls during the tremor, they were too astounded to move as it was their first experience.

b. The fellow workers were infuriated**:** their hands **having clutched** wooden planks or metal rods, they were heading for the assailants' construction site.

c. The teenager was bawling out for his usual breakfast – his tantrum **getting** worse since his refusal to leave his bedroom.

d. The illegal hawkers panicked, grabbing only the precious goods – the environmental officers were approaching in a van, a police patrol car **following** close behind.

## EXERCISE 2: SENTENCE-WRITING (2)

**Construct five sentences** of your own content for **each of the following structures:**
(a)  3 Verbs + 2 Participle Phrases
(b)  1 Verb + 3 Prepositional Phrases + 2 Participle Phrases

Examples:

a. **Having splashed** all his money in the karaoke lounge, the tipsy executive *bade* farewell to his companions, *trod* out of the noisy refuge and *plodded* *the long journey back, **anticipating** a bashing from his nagging wife at home.*

b. ***Having illuminated*** *the room with torchlight, the curious pair <u>stumbled</u> across a messy floor, <u>peered</u> into a large cupboard and <u>rummaged</u> through old clothes, books and toys, **amusing** themselves with the unusual discovery.*

c. ***Having triggered*** *an alarm in the bungalow, the burglar <u>scrambled</u> <u>out of</u> the bedroom, <u>down</u> the staircase and <u>out through</u> the window, **staying** as low as possible to avoid being seen.*

d. ***Having recognized*** *the arsonist, the grey-haired retiree <u>shuffled</u> <u>away from</u> him, <u>across</u> a car park and <u>towards</u> the neighbourhood police post, **intending** to report him.*

## EXERCISE 3: PARAGRAPH-WRITING

**Write <u>one</u> Conversation of <u>six</u> paragraphs using at least <u>five</u> Nominative Absolutes with either of the Participle Phrases.** Follow the Narrative Essay-Writing guideline as close as possible.

PART 3: **CONVERSATION** (6 paragraphs in about 150 words)
Describe only significant facts that developed an understanding of the issue as revealed by the characters.
    (i)    Use Inverted Commas.
    (j)    Use Nominative Absolutes with Participle Phrases.
    (k)    Use any Present and Future Tenses in the speeches.
    (l)    Use Conditional Clauses in the speeches if possible.
    (m)    Use Simple Past and Past Continuous Tenses in the narration.

Paragraph 1: Introduce the situation involving characters, location and purpose for this conversation. One or two sentences will suffice with some Participle Phrases or Clauses.

Paragraph 2:

> "Don't disturb me!" bellowed the irritated pupil, his eyes glaring at the bullies.

Paragraph 3:

> One culprit, their abuse halted by the sudden appearance of the class monitress, retorted, "Here comes your heroine." The timid boy having escaped their grasp at that instant, the three students returned to their seats.

Paragraph 4:

> "If I had not intervened," asserted the spectacled girl, her approach being both sympathetic and firm, "you would have suffered in their hands again. You must learn to stand up for yourself."

Paragraph 5:

> "Unless you were I," responded the timid boy, "you could not understand." Being warned by his father not to get into trouble in the new school, he had to comply as he himself was a bully in a previous school.

[For paragraphs 2, 3, 4 and 5, actual examples of how to write a variety of inverted commas are given including relevant narration related to each speech.]

Paragraph 6: Show how characters left the scene to end the conversation.

Here is an example adapted from the notes to illustrate the use of Participle Phrases and Nominative Absolutes:

**Example:**

> It was a suicidal mission. The lone policeman ambled confidently forward, <u>the armed mob **blocking** the route out of the province</u>.

"Who is the village head here? Who is the leader?" **inquired** Sammy, **having raised** his hands in front of them to show that he was not carrying any weapon.

A heavily bearded man, <u>his eyes **glaring** at the uniformed figure</u>, **bellowed**, "I am the village head. Who are these people behind you?"

"They are innocent villagers," **explained** the calm officer, "whose homes have been destroyed. They are not fighters. They simply want to leave this place, <u>everyone **having abandoned** their village</u>. There's no point harming these frightened people. You can observe that there are old people, women and children with them." <u>His lips **having paused** for a moment</u>, Sammy gazed into the eyes of the old man, **praying** he would let them through.

"Tell them we don't want them back here," **warned** the fiery leader, **heightening** his voice to ensure his demand was heard. "They will get hurt if they come back. Then they cannot blame us."

<u>The village head **exerting** his authority</u>, the armed mob stepped aside for the convoy of vehicles to pass through. Sammy thanked the wise leader profusely before taking the last vehicle away from the troubled scene.

# EXERCISE 4: ESSAY-WRITING

**Write one narrative essay of 500 words** from the following:

1. A hijack.
2. Death at a train station.
3. Describe a possible experience of a drug addict.
4. Describe your bad experiences with household pests.
5. Describe your visit to an unusual place.

Alternatively, if you prefer, choose one factual essay below instead:

1. Do people need a religion?
2. Filial piety.
3. Describe the kinds of prejudice that may exist in your country.
4. Should people get married?
5. How do you know what is right or wrong?

# ASSIGNMENT 8

(Submit these exercises for marking and evaluation. Write all your answers on A4 size single-lined papers.)

## EXERCISE 1: FACTUAL ESSAY-WRITING

Transform each underlined sentence in the following essay into Participle Phrase or Nominative Absolute, changing the content or structure as necessary.

### ARE HUMANS RESPONSIBLE FOR THEIR OWN MISERIES TODAY?

The world today is better in terms of a higher standard of living: people can expect more goods and better quality of services modernized by high technology in which the rich countries are receiving more than the poor ones. However, human greed for power and money and human craving for drugs and sex are causing miseries round the globe. These facts are undeniable and broadcast almost daily in newspapers.

The rich and middle classes, because they desire more wealth or more leisure activities with their strong purchasing power, are too busy to care for more babies. The populations of rich countries are stagnating or declining; the poor countries are increasing their birth rate. The rich nations have to resolve its labour shortage by getting more foreign help but they are risking the import of undesirable elements.

Too many people in poor countries who are relying on meagre wages, less medical benefits and few technological aids from donor countries simply survive in austerity. Others migrate legally or illegally to rich countries. They crave for a better life for themselves and their families. However, criminal syndicates cheat many workers of hard earned cash with job promises or lead many females into prostitution.

Human corruption through briberies and extortions wreaks havoc in the rich commercial world. The poor are also suffering from land grabbing authorities and failure or delay to get official licensing for business without costly payments. While tyranny of the masses is existing through individual or group dictatorship or dogmatic religious policies are peeking its head, human corruption knows no boundary through its thirst for power too.

Rich countries have invested in research and development of higher technology. The world becomes destabilized when these nations grow in both economic and military strengths, as they have the capacity to subdue weaker nations. Unilateral action by such country to take over the sovereignty of a weaker nation is a fearful likelihood so that current conflicts and threats of war possibly can exacerbate to full blown wars.

Sadly, governments of poor countries are ignoring the plight of their poor in order to boost up military power. Famines due to droughts, floods or locust attacks can easily wipe out villages without modern facilities. Natural disasters like tsunami or earthquake render these governments helpless in terms of humanitarian aid because rich countries suspect them of siphoning off aid for their own armies. Help eventually arrives when trustworthy news gets out to the world but often too late. Death of the poor victims are becoming acceptable because of human apathy.

A few industrial countries assume that they will have the technology to repair the ozone layer in the future whereas the greenhouse effect is raising sea levels and changing climate by warming the ocean water; some countries exploit the natural reserves when major ecological damage to water and land and extinction of species of plants and animals are irreparable. Humans are losing their habitats as a result.

Cash crops of drugs are growing in the remote areas of the countrysides. Effective networking by traffickers has created an unstoppable distribution channel to modern cities round the world. Some governments have capitulated to its onslaught, so drug-fixing centres are permitted to control the situation; other governments are still prevailing against drugs, so the death penalty and confiscation of drug-related assets provide deterrence. However, the lure of huge immediate profit captivates unconscionable human greed when senseless addicts are foregoing wealth or committing crime to feed their habit.

Sexual diseases especially AIDS or Acquired Immune Deficiency Syndrome are rampant. They affect all countries, some greater than others, when tourists are seeking sex from prostitutes and people are engaging in promiscuity. Researchers believe that millions of humans are carrying sexual diseases like herpes without realizing it especially a type of herpes that can be easily transmitted through kissing, which causes deformities in childbirth. An insidious epidemic is scary but real.

<u>Many other human miseries are existing like physical illnesses through gluttony, lack of exercise or alcoholism, mental stresses from difficulties in job, study, romance or the family, social issues of racial riots or religious conflicts, and moral degradation in the killings of innocent lives through terrorism or in the abuses of citizens by the removal of human rights.</u>  Humans are the cause of their own miseries.

<u>Humans have easily perceived their own flaws in economic losses such as retrenchments, bankruptcies, business failures, stock losses and currency crises</u>.  Instead of blaming God, evolution, fate or even aliens, humans must recognize they are responsible for their own miseries.  <u>They must collaborate locally and across national boundaries to arrest their own misdeeds.</u>  Blind nationalism is simply digging one's head in the grave.  Current individual apathy is designing a bleak world for our children in the near future.


## EXERCISE 2:  NARRATIVE ESSAY-WRITING

The narrative essay allows you to display a wide variety of advanced grammar structures.  Follow the guideline closely unless you are quite confident in writing your own style.

**Write <u>one</u> narrative essay of 500 words** from the following:

1. Write a comical story about life in an army camp.
2. Describe an experience when you were living or travelling far away from modern conveniences.
3. Describe an experience of a door-to-door salesman.
4. Write one possible realistic scenario as a story in which the world might end.
5. Write a realistic story of how a fugitive finally met his fate.

# EXERCISE 3: FACTUAL ESSAY-WRITING

The factual essay grades more on content though good language is still essential. So displaying advanced grammar structures depends on your resourcefulness. Just ensure that each paragraph shows different advanced structures in different locations as appropriate.

**Write one factual essay of 500 words** from the following:

1. Why are countries keen on space research and exploration?
2. You have three months to live. How will you spend this time?
3. How will you spend your money if you have a million dollars?
4. What possible new inventions do you like to have?
5. Describe a natural disaster.

# VOCABULARY LISTS

For narrative essays, simply memorize the vocabularies that you need most often instead of helplessly trying to digest the whole dictionary. Below are some very useful lists that you can practise for your assignments too:

## "WALK" VERBS.

The "Walk" verbs are useful in Suspense and Climax. The words are arranged in their Simple Present, Simple Past, Present Participle, and Past Participle forms with their meanings.

**amble, ambled, ambling, ambled**....walk slowly in a relaxed manner
**gad, gadded, gadding, gadded**....wander about idly
**gallivant, gallivanted, gallivanting, gallivanted**....roam for pleasure
**glide, glided, gliding, glided**.... move smoothly and effortlessly
**hike, hiked, hiking, hiked**....take a long walk
**hobble, hobbled, hobbling, hobbled**....walk painfully along with both feet hurt usually
**idle, idled, idling, idled**....move aimlessly, doing nothing
**limp, limped, limping, limped**....walk with difficulty because a foot or leg is hurt
**meander, meandered, meandering, meandered**....travel slowly not in any particular direction
**mince, minced, mincing, minced**....walk quickly in small steps like a Japanese lady in kimono
**pace, paced, pacing, paced** ...walk anxiously within a small area usually while waiting
**plod, plodded, plodding, plodded**....walk slowly as if the feet are too heavy to lift up easily
**prance, pranced, prancing, pranced**....march along with exaggerated movements
**promenade, promenaded, promenading, promenaded**....walk for pleasure especially shopping
**prowl, prowled, prowling, prowled**....loiter around in a place especially without permission
**ramble, rambled, rambling, rambled**....take a long walk to explore
**reel, reeled, reeling, reeled**....walk unsteadily as if about to fall
**roam, roamed, roaming, roamed**....wander without a particular purpose

**saunter, sauntered, sauntering, sauntered**....walk casually
**scamper, scampered, scampering, scampered**....run with small quick, bouncing steps
**scurry, scurried, scurrying, scurried**... .run in a quick, hurrying movement with sound of footsteps
**shamble, shambled, shambling, shambled**....walk carelessly and heavily, dragging feet while bending body forward slightly
**shuffle, shuffled, shuffling, shuffled**....walk by dragging the feet slightly along the ground
**slink, slunk, slinking, slunk**....walk slowly and secretively to avoid being seen
**slither, slithered, slithering, slithered**....slide in an uneven manner
**slouch, slouched, slouching, slouched**....walk tiredly with head and shoulders drooping
**stagger, staggered, staggering, staggered**....walk unsteadily along
**stalk, stalked, stalking, stalked**....walk stiffly, proudly or angrily
**stamp, stamped, stamping, stamped**....walk angrily by hitting the feet on the floor
**step, stepped, stepping, stepped**....lift the foot and put it down
**straggle, straggled, straggling, straggled**....wandered behind or away from a group
**stride, strode, striding, stridden**....walk hurriedly with long steps •
**stroll, strolled, strolling, strolled**....walk slowly in a relaxed manner
**strut, strutted, strutting, strutted**....walk proudly
**stumble, stumbled, stumbling, stumbled**....walk unsteadily particularly after a clumsy step
**swagger, swaggered, swaggering, swaggered**....walk proudly with body upright, swinging the hips
**tiptoe, tiptoed, tiptoeing, tiptoed**....walk very quietly on your toes
**toddle, toddled, toddling, toddled**....walk unsteadily in quick short steps like a child
**tramp, tramped, tramping, tramped**....walk for a long distance in a particular direction
**tread, trod, treading, trodden**.....walk carefully in a particular direction
**trip, tripped, tripping, tripped**... .walk lightly and quickly usually on high heels
**trudge, trudged, trudging, trudged**....walk tiredly with slow steps
**waddle, waddled, waddling, waddled**....walk in short quick steps, swaying the hips
**wend, wended, wending, wended**....walk slowly and cautiously, avoiding obstacles

# "TOUCH" VERBS

The "Touched" verbs are useful in Suspense and Climax. The words are in Past Participle forms for use in the Perfect and Passive Tenses though most of them are similar to the Simple Past forms. Active-Perfect Participle Phrases need them especially. Their meanings are next to them.

| | | |
|---|---|---|
| **brandished** | : | waved threateningly or triumphantly |
| **bumped** | : | knocked into someone or something |
| **caressed** | : | stroked gently |
| **clasped** | : | held together firmly |
| **clinched** | : | held securely |
| **clutched** | : | held firmly |
| **crinkled** | : | caused to make wrinkles or a rustling sound |
| **crumbled** | : | broken into crumbs or fragments |
| **cuddled** | : | held close |
| **cuffed** | : | struck with the open hand |
| **dandled** | : | moved (a child) up and down on the knee |
| **elbowed** | : | shoved with the elbow |
| **embraced** | : | hugged in the arms |
| **extirpated** | : | uprooted |
| **fondled** | : | touched tenderly |
| **grappled** | : | gripped especially while in a struggle |
| **grasped** | : | gripped firmly |
| **impelled** | : | pushed into motion |
| **jostled** | : | pushed roughly |
| **lacerated** | : | torn jaggedly |
| **nipped** | : | compressed between the thumb and a finger |
| **nudged** | : | pushed gently especially with the elbow to get attention |
| **nuzzled** | : | rubbed gently with the nose |
| **pinched** | : | pressed tightly between the thumb and a finger |
| **pricked** | : | pierced a small hole or caused a piercing sensation |
| **prodded** | : | poked with a sharp object |
| **racked** | : | shaken violently |
| **rent** | : | torn with violent force |
| **ripped** | : | torn violently or roughly |
| **rived** | : | torn apart (to shreds) |
| **shoved** | : | pushed roughly or violently |
| **smacked** | : | slapped forcibly or loudly |
| **spanked** | : | slapped the buttocks |
| **strained** | : | stretched tight |

| | | |
|---|---|---|
| **swiped** | : | hit hard with a sweeping blow |
| **swished** | : | caused to move with a whistling or hissing sound |
| **thumped** | : | beat heavily |
| **tussled** | : | struggled in a vigorous way |
| **tweaked** | : | twisted with a sharp or sudden movement |
| **wielded** | : | handled a tool or weapon |
| **wrenched** | : | given a sudden or violent pull or twist to remove |
| **wrested** | : | taken away by violent pulling or twisting |
| **wrestled** | : | held in a struggle |
| **wrung** | : | twisted forcibly |
| **yanked** | : | pulled with a sharp movement or jerk |

# "LOOK" VERBS

The "Look" verbs are useful in Suspense and Climax. The words are given in Present Participle forms. Active-Continuous Participle Phrases need them especially. Their meanings are next to them.

| | | |
|---|---|---|
| **discerning** | : | seeing something that was not readily apparent |
| **gaping** | : | staring in open-mouthed astonishment |
| **gazing** | : | looking steadily with prolonged attention |
| **glancing** | : | looking indifferently or hastily |
| **glaring** | : | staring with a fixed piercing gaze |
| **glimpsing** | : | catching a quick view, noticing something |
| **gloating** | : | staring malignantly or with uncaring satisfaction |
| **glowering** | : | looking angrily with hostile expression |
| **inspecting** | : | looking critically to find errors or flaws |
| **leering** | : | casting sidelong looks that were lustful |
| **noticing** | : | becoming aware of something already present but not seen |
| **ogling** | : | casting amorous glances intended to be inviting |
| **peeking** | : | looking shyly with reluctance or playfully with occasional hidings |
| **peeping** | : | looking curiously through a small opening without permission |
| **peering** | : | looking with difficulty as if nearsighted or under dim light |
| **perceiving** | : | obtaining understanding through the eyes |
| **poring** | : | studying something intently |
| **scanning** | : | examining point by point with a wide vision or, colloquially, looking over something hastily like a newspaper |
| **scrutinizing** | : | examining closely and critically |
| **squinting** | : | looking through partially closed eyelids because of glare, poor vision or laughter |
| **surveying** | : | securing a general view |

# "SAY" VERBS

The "Say" verbs are primarily useful in Conversation besides Suspense and Climax. The words are given in Simple Past forms. Their meanings are next to them.

| | | |
|---|---|---|
| **accented** | : | stressed |
| **accentuated** | : | heightened the stress |
| **admonished** | : | warned by expressing disapproval |
| **alleged** | : | said something is true without proof |
| **assailed** | : | assaulted with words |
| **asserted** | : | stated firmly that something was true |
| **assuaged** | : | offered words to relieve from suffering (also lessened) |
| **avowed** | : | declared |
| **babbled** | : | talked in a confused and excited way |
| **belittled** | : | lessened the importance of |
| **bellowed** | : | shouted in a loud, deep voice |
| **berated** | : | accused strongly |
| **blasphemed** | : | spoke against God |
| **blurted** | : | said out suddenly |
| **broached** | : | brought in a new subject |
| **carped** | : | talked complainingly |
| **chattered** | : | talked quickly and continuously about common things |
| **chortled** | : | laughed as one is pleased |
| **chuckled** | : | laughed quietly |
| **censured** | : | criticized by one with authority |
| **coaxed** | : | pleaded to gain one's end |
| **condoned** | : | forgave a serious offence |
| **contended** | : | argued against |
| **contradicted** | : | declared that a statement was untrue |
| **decried** | : | condemned with intent to discredit |
| **deplored** | : | expressed keen regret |
| **derided** | : | mocked |
| **differentiated** | : | contrasted or pointed out the differences |
| **disavowed** | : | denied any connection with |
| **dissuaded** | : | swayed others to change their view |
| **distorted** | : | twisted the truth |
| **drawled** | : | spoke slowly, especially sleepily, lengthening the sounds |
| **droned** | : | talked boringly in a low, monotonous voice |
| **elucidated** | : | made clearly intelligible |
| **embellished** | : | added interesting or fictitious details |

| | | |
|---|---|---|
| **enumerated** | : | explained in great detail |
| **expounded** | : | gave a clear and detailed explanation formally |
| **felicitated** | : | expressed happiness over another's success |
| **flattered** | : | praised to satisfy another's vanity |
| **foretold** | : | predicted |
| **gibbered** | : | talked very fast confusedly because of fear or madness |
| **gushed** | : | expressed praise or pleasure in an exaggerated insincere way |
| **growled** | : | said in a low, rough and rather angry voice |
| **haggled** | : | bargained |
| **heckled** | : | badgered with questions or comments |
| **impugned** | : | attacked the honesty of the statement or person |
| **imputed** | : | blamed |
| **incited** | : | stirred up |
| **interceded** | : | tried to reconcile differences |
| **interposed** | : | interrupted with a comment |
| **jabbered** | : | talked very quickly and excitedly |
| **lamented** | : | expressed discontent |
| **moaned** | : | said unhappily or anxiously |
| **mollified** | : | appeased |
| **mumbled** | : | spoke indistinctly |
| **murmured** | : | said quietly and not easily heard |
| **muttered** | : | complained very softly |
| **paraphrased** | : | interpreted |
| **parried** | : | evaded |
| **persisted** | : | continued resolutely |
| **pledged** | : | promised |
| **prated** | : | talked foolishly, boastfully or insolently |
| **prattled** | : | talked about unimportant things for the sake of talking |
| **rambled** | : | talked in a confused and illogical manner |
| **rebutted** | : | contradicted with evidence |
| **reiterate** | : | repeated continually |
| **retorted** | : | responded in a retaliatory manner |
| **scoffed** | : | showed contempt by teasing |
| **shrieked** | : | screamed at a high-pitched note |
| **slandered** | : | injured one's reputation |
| **solicited** | : | asked with earnestness |
| **soliloquized** | : | talked to oneself |
| **sputtered** | : | spoke with some struggle, coughing out words |
| **stammered** | : | spoke hesitatingly, repeating words or sounds |
| **thundered** | : | said loudly and forcefully because of anger |

Made in the USA
San Bernardino, CA
24 January 2016